BUILDING A SHARED VISION

BUILDING
A SHARED
VISION

A LEADER'S GUIDE
TO ALIGNING
THE ORGANIZATION

C. PATRICK LEWIS

PRODUCTIVITY PRESS
Portland, Oregon

Additional copies of this book are available from the publisher. Discounts are available for multiple copies through the Sales Department (800-394-6868). Address all other inquiries to:

Productivity, Inc.
P.O. Box 13390
Portland OR 97213-0390
United States of America
Telephone: 503-235-0600
Telefax: 503-235-0909
E-mail: service@productivityinc.com

Cover and text design by Bill Stanton
Cover Illustration by Victor Sadowski
Page composition by William H. Brunson, Typography Services
Printed and bound by Edwards Brothers in the United States of America

Library of Congress Cataloging-in-Publication Data

Lewis, C. Patrick (Carl Patrick)
    Building a shared vision : a leader's guide to aligning the
organization / C. Patrick Lewis
        p. cm.
    Includes bibliographical references.
    ISBN 1-56327-163-X
      1. Organizational change—Forecasting.   2. Strategic planning.
    3. Organizational change—Problems, exercises, etc.   4. Strategic
    planning—Problems, exercises.   I. Title.
    HD58.8.L49 1996
    658.4'063—dc20   96-43390
                                                                CIP

02 01 00 99   10 9 8 7 6 5 4 3 2

To Barbara, my wife,
for the love and joy she brings to our lives,
and Michael and Cameron, our sons,
for their happiness and inspiration.

Table of Contents

PART II: METHODOLOGY FOR VISION DEVELOPMENT

PART III: ORGANIZATIONAL VISIONING ASSESSMENTS

Publisher's Acknowledgments

C. PATRICK LEWIS has turned many successful years of teaching organizational visioning into a step-by-step method that can be easily assimilated and manifested by the enthusiastic reader. We thank him for his decision to publish his fine method with Productivity Press. Special thanks to Diane Asay, editor in chief of Productivity Press, for her guidance in shaping a user friendly book that integrates a variety of vision building materials into an interconnected plan. Thanks to Mary A. Junewick for managing book production, Tim Hickey for sales planning, Mary Bradley for publicity, Julie Zinkus for copyediting, Lydia Junewick for proofreading, William H. Brunson, Typography Services for page composition, and Susan Swanson for print managing. Special thanks also to Bill Stanton for outstanding page and cover design.

How to Use This Book

FOR OVER 30 YEARS C. Patrick Lewis has applied his knowledge and skills to a wide variety of organization, management, and leadership issues. This book, *Building a Shared Vision*, compiles his experience in helping companies build an organizational vision. As such, it goes far beyond books that simply define visioning or tell you why it is important to your organization. This book systematizes visioning into a deliberate, easy-to-follow, step-by-step process. As a consultant, Mr. Lewis guides companies through the visioning process with several learning techniques and tools. In this book, Mr. Lewis shares his techniques and tools so that anyone in the organization who assumes the leadership or facilitation role, will have all the necessary materials with which to achieve a successful organizational vision.

Part I, Organizational Visioning, is a comprehensive discussion of how to build a shared vision. It gives a brief historical context and tells the *what, why, where*, and *who* of visioning. The *how* of visioning is explained in six vision building phases. Finally, the key points of Part I are summarized. Throughout Part I, the text is coordinated with Parts III and IV of the book by means of clipboard and slide icons shown in the margins. The icons are provided to help the visioning leader or facilitator give an integrated visual presentation and conduct an integrated assessment process.

Part II, Methodology for Vision Development, presents the six vision building phases in six succinct, easy-to-follow charts. The steps and activities that are essential to each phase are listed. If these lists are followed, one step will build sensibly upon another and nothing important will be forgotten. The steps and activities have been coordinated to Parts III and IV of the book. The Support Tools column of each chart shows which assessments or overheads apply.

Part III, Organizational Visioning Assessments, furnishes nine detailed questionnaires that are essential to the visioning process. These questionnaires help assess the present thinking of the organization, measure the alignment among those in the organization, and, very importantly, involve everyone in the organization—thereby ensuring that the process and the ensuing vision are shared. These forms may be considered templates from which to create your own customized forms.

Part IV, Visual Presentation, contains a complete overhead presentation of the material in Part I. The visioning leader or facilitator can use these examples to create overheads to enhance the presentation of the visioning process. Overheads will aid assimilation of the concepts and will stimulate and encourage questions and discussion—again ensuring that the process, as well as the ensuing vision, are shared.

Part V has been compiled so that the individual, the team, or the unit may apply the larger company visioning process to more localized and specific goals. This section repeats some of the key ideas of Part I and also reworks them as the reader is taken again through the six *how* phases of building the vision.

Note: The assessment forms and overheads in this book may be copied and/or adapted for use in your organization. The author and editors welcome your feedback about any parts of this book. If sufficient interest is expressed, the publisher will create and package full size forms and overheads to be offered for use with this book. As always, Productivity Press is committed to offering you the very best in materials to enhance the way you do business and ensure your prosperity.

PART I

ORGANIZATIONAL VISIONING

CHAPTER 1

Building a Shared Vision

IN THE 1950s, it was management by objectives (MBO) followed in the mid-1960s by strategic planning that were acclaimed as the vital tools for corporate and governmental management. For four decades they either independently or jointly mesmerized many organizations looking for help with identifying weaknesses and strengths, gauging the competition, and evaluating the business and economic climate. All of this was followed by attempts to develop and implement strategies and goals that would maximize the use of that data.

Although both MBO and strategic planning became popular management tools, the results soon began to raise questions as to the real effectiveness of either planning process. Despite serving a logical purpose, by the early 1970s leaders of organizations that were applying these tools began to detect problems. Executives and managers noticed an erosion of individual commitment, a loss of interest in change, and an abrupt growth of divisive internal politics. The planning process had degenerated into highly politicized games. But, even more important, a growing number of leaders complained that both planning processes had a negative effect on what many of them believed was an extremely valuable management philosophy and tool—vision.

THE DRIVING FORCE

Vision gives expression to where the organization wants to go and how to get there.

By the early 1970s, a growing cadre of leaders recognized that it is vision, personal and organizational, that provides the strategic element that is too often missing when their organizations discuss goals, objectives, and performance. They discovered that while strategic planning was supposed to orient them to the future, their strategic plans focused more on current problems than on tomorrow's opportunities. They admitted that their strategy focused more on short-term earnings than on long-term gains. This was an important admission, since determining long-term strategy requires synthesis and vision. After all, vision is what determines and gives expression to where an organization wants to go and how it intends to get there. For many executives, vision has provided the driving force needed to bring the members of their organizations together in the achievement of future goals and strategies.

NEW REALITIES

Meanwhile, however, the 1970s and 1980s saw the economic and financial world turn upside down. Once-stable markets and industries fell victim to global competition. The American workplace was all but overcome by foreign investments. At the same time, information technology dramatically altered the meaning and application of leadership and power within the corporation. Business and industrial leaders found themselves at the vanguard of extremely rapid and unpredictable change. Unfortunately, many of them were overzealous in their response to the new realities. Somehow they wanted to believe that the transformations challenging America—economic, technical, political, and social—made history and its lessons irrelevant. It was easy—perhaps too easy—to assume that the new realities demanded revolutionary changes in management assumptions, values, philosophies, and tools.

As a consequence, leadership began what we can characterize as a frenzied reengineering of everything. Along the way organizations began to experiment with and integrate into their reengineering efforts such concepts and tools as excellence, quality, continuous improvement, learning organizations, empowerment, and teams. This experimentation was motivated, of course, by their struggle for survival in a global environment, in which the only constant was the exponential speed of change.

LOOKING TO THE FUTURE

What caught and continues to hold the attention of executives is a steady stream of books, articles, scholarly journals, newspaper columns, and speeches that examine problems and provide solutions to the current and future challenges facing their organizations. Too often, however, they send incomplete or misleading messages. They omit any recognition that success depends on the ability of corporate leadership to look to the future through a shared vision. It should be an integral part of a list of current change strategies that range from the incremental improvements promised by total quality management, continuous improvement, and process management to the more dramatic improvements predicted by the implementation of learning organizations, knowledge-based organizations, business process reengineering, or horizontal organizations.

Although their methodologies differ, most of these change strategies have two common elements:

- They focus on manufacturing and the shift from competing on *what* is being made to *how* it is being made.

- They concentrate heavily on incremental improvements in quality, on redesigning internal processes, on restructuring, and in many cases, distancing workers from consideration.

Of course, these and numerous other spin-off strategies have improved competitiveness. We will remember them, however, as introductory responses to an era of reinvention and revolutionary change. In this environment we have been urged to hold nothing sacred and to reengineer everything, to respond to an insane world with our own brand of insanity.

Survival and success in an unforgiving competitive environment hinges on an inspired shared vision and the achievement of operational excellence by doing things right.

WHAT DO WE WANT TO CREATE?

A change strategy without a direct link to shared vision significantly increases the potential for failure.

In today's economy leaders must ask more than how we can redeploy assets and rethink operational strategy in response to our competitive environment. They must create the vision and the organization that can lead people where they want to go, despite their not knowing it yet. Far more significant questions focus on what we want to create and how we can come up with new ways to serve our customers. As corporate upheaval escalates, current estimates suggest that at least half the organizations attempting to restructure around processes alone will encounter serious and unexpected problems and risk failure. Clearly, the implementation of a change strategy, by any label, without a direct link to a shared vision of direction significantly increases the potential for failure for even a well-run organization.

As important as improvement processes are to organizational success, of greater significance is the strategic issue of direction or vision. Direction setting is identifying the *where*; its intent is to make certain that everyone in the organization works toward the achievement of the same goals. Processes are the *how*; their purpose is to assure that things get done efficiently and effectively. Based on experience, a growing number of executives are admitting that improving the success rate in companies implementing change processes requires dynamic, shared vision. Its role is significantly more powerful than the typical leader of an organization realizes. Vision pulls the organization toward the future, based on an image of how that future may appear. It gives the organization a clear and exciting reason for the effort required to achieve something important. The vision must be built on improved communication, awareness of the problems, adaptability in the face of volatile circumstances, and knowledge of the product and the customer. It has become clear to many leaders that improvement and managerial planning processes are inadequate substitutes for visioning. As a result, they now emphasize in their recruitment of executives and managers the need for visionaries capable of understanding the business and its potential in a dynamic world. Vision is more valuable today and will become even more so tomorrow than the management styles and change processes popularized in recent years.

The critical task, today's executives argue, starts with weaving all that needs to be done into a single shared vision of what we want to create.

It is more than just a little ironic that an organization moving to implement the desired operational and process improvements, without directing itself at the right new tomorrow, may only be putting itself on an even faster track to failure.

Why is a shared vision so important? What exactly is a shared vision and how does an organization make it happen? How does an organization succeed in developing a vision-building process that wins the participation of its members? Significantly, a number of business and organization leaders have expressed their frustration in getting a handle on what vision is. Although they constantly confront such words as mission, purpose, strategy, and values, many still look for ways to get around the word maze and create a shared vision for the organization. The following outline provides a framework for a discussion of these and related questions and describes the mechanics of a process that can provide any organization with a shared vision and the means to translate it into reality:

"Vision is the art of seeing things invisible."

—Jonathan Swift

- What is shared vision?

- Why do it?

- Where do you begin?

- What are the roles people play?

- What are the key elements?

CHAPTER 2

What Is Shared Vision?

WHAT IS A SHARED VISION and what does it look like? The very
word—*vision*—arouses a wide array of appealing images. In our minds,
these images represent exceptional achievement, values and beliefs
that bond, challenging and even audacious goals, and even the reasons
for the organization's existence. Vision is something that demands an
organization's best efforts. It's appealing, nice, great, but what exactly
is it? A shared vision is a statement that answers the question, "What
do we want to create?" and captures an ideal, unique, and attractive
image of an organization's future. It provides focus and energy to what
the leadership wants the organization to be and inspires a commitment from everyone to achieve it. A shared vision is a compelling por-
trait of a promised land that inspires enthusiasm and excitement in
people when they come to work. That is what distinguishes shared
vision from mission, strategy, and values. The organization's mission
determines what people do when they arrive at their workplace. It
answers the question "Why do we exist?" The organization's strategy
responds to how they will do it. Finally, values provide a critical guide
for interactions and relationships with staff, peers, customers, vendors,
and all other stakeholders.

Shared vision provides focus and energy to what leadership wants the organization to be and inspires a commitment from everyone to achieve it.

6–7

In an easily understood and inspiring statement, a shared vision presents a clear picture of where everyone agrees the organization is going and how it intends to get there. A shared vision is an expression of direction and hope. If, however, there is no hope, it is difficult to create a shared vision.

A FEW POWERFUL EXAMPLES

A few examples can illustrate the power and value of a shared vision. Bill Gates remains committed to his vision: "A computer on every desk and in every home, all running Microsoft software." It was Walt Disney's vision that resulted in the reinvention of the concept of an amusement park. For years the vision at Apple Computer, Inc. was "the bringing of computer power to the people." The need for quality improvement at Ford Motor Corporation inspired the vision statement, "Quality Is Job 1." At Saturn the vision was and still is to reassert the ability of American workers to produce a high quality automobile at a low cost. By helping "a girl reach her highest potential," the Girl Scouts successfully redirected their vision away from traditional household skills to activities that reflect today's opportunities for women in science, business, and technology.

Other examples of powerful shared visions include McDonald's concept of "Service, Cleanliness, Quality, Values;" Federal Express' "guaranteed overnight delivery of letters and small parcels;" and the Johnson and Johnson commitment to products only for "mothers, nurses, doctors, and patients." The vision in Toyota's Lexus division resulted in the invention of a new luxury car and a new standard for luxury service. At ServiceMaster, the commitment is to sell back to people chunks of their own leisure time. They do things for people they dislike doing for themselves. The vision that differentiates Southwest Airlines is its focus on service, cost control, and price. Its people, culture, marketing, operations, and distribution processes reflect a total commitment to their vision.

DEFINITION AND FRAMEWORK

In addition to identifying and defining the new tomorrow, a shared vision provides the framework that guides all decision making, planning, and action. In today's environment organizations are finding success, and even their existence, extremely difficult without reference to a shared vision that everyone from key executives to first-level personnel buys into. Everything from the structure of the organization to leadership style, management methods, and action plans is designed to support a shared vision. It can transform and reshape an organization from products and services to production and distribution. For a vision to have such impact, however, it must be well understood and shared by all of the organization's key people. A shared vision is more than simply a tool; it is an essential strategy, the organization's culture, and a mindset for stretching dreams about what an organization can be.

Shared vision provides the framework that guides all decision making, planning, and action.

ORGANIZATIONAL STRENGTHS

A shared vision focuses on the organizational strengths and resources that must be developed to achieve an ideal that by definition is always just beyond reach. It is the creative force that drives the never-ending quest for success and greatness. For the people of an organization, a shared vision provides motivation, meaning, and direction for work. People feel drawn to a shared vision. To work toward its achievement confirms the essence of success and value to their lives and the future of the organization.

It is the creative force that drives the never-ending quest for success and greatness.

Although this is often unsaid, people seek something beyond money and ego as reasons for their work. "When there is no vision, the people perish." (Proverbs, chapter 29, verse 18). The same can be said of an organization. A shared vision connects people to an important undertaking and gives them and the organization something for which to take a stand.

A shared vision can transform an organization and reshape every step of product or service research and development, production, and distribution. Without a vision of the future an organization is never going to do everything that needs to be done to succeed. Now and in the future, vision will be more valuable than the management tools and styles popularized in the past twenty or so years. The truth is, visioning is much more than a powerful tool: it is a strategy, culture, and mental attitude for expanding the organization's horizons about what can be. This is a significant achievement during a time when product after product looks, feels, and smells like all the others.

CHAPTER 3

Why Do It?

DOES THE "RIGHT" SHARED VISION really make a difference? Are leaders correct in their belief that nothing happens until there is a shared vision? What does a persuasive and inspiring shared vision contribute to the survival and success of an organization? How will leadership taking on such a task and test benefit the organization and its people? Keep in mind that a profitable business can be created without a vision and there are plenty of examples. But, if your goal is more than to make a lot of money—if you want to build a great company or organization—a vision is vital.

THE DREAM REALIZED

From Henry Ford to Walt Disney, from Steven Jobs and Steve Wozniak to Bill Gates—it would be impossible to imagine their accomplishments without a vision. In each case, while the company was still small, they clearly articulated and instilled a vision. From the Model T Ford to spreadsheets, this country has a history of being open to innovators—people with vision. For companies, like Wal-Mart, Ben and Jerry's Homemade, Microsoft, and Mrs. Field's Cookies, betting on an

"If you can dream it,

you can do it."

—Walt Disney

inspired vision provided the direction that resulted in the realization of a dream. Vision is what these companies are all about. In addition, their visions changed the competition. Consider for a moment the revolutionary impact of Federal Express' initial vision statement that "We will deliver the package by 10:30 the next morning." In each instance, these companies recognized that if you fail to innovate and shape your organization's future and direction, someone or something else will.

THE JAPANESE EXAMPLE

The real miracle of "Japanese Management" was their ability to develop, communicate, and implement a grand shared vision.

There has been an even greater appreciation of vision in Japan. Any explanation of the ascendancy of Japanese firms in the past thirty years would be flawed without recognizing and understanding the contribution of their visions to their global success. An analysis of that phenomenon reveals that the real miracle of "Japanese Management" was due less to quality circles and participative management than it was to their ability to develop, communicate, and implement a grand shared vision.

For example, Tokyo Tsushin Kogyo, known today as Sony Corporation, went from a maker of cheap transistor radios to a world leader in electronic entertainment equipment. For founder, Masaru Ibuka, the company could achieve greatness only with a bold and compelling vision. "To create a product that becomes pervasive worldwide" was the successfully developed and implemented result at Sony. In 1970, who would have believed that Honda, at that time a third-rate producer by any standard, would deliver more cars of higher quality to American buyers than Chrysler in fifteen years? The vision at Honda and other Japanese auto companies pushed them to develop an almost endless array of new competitive strategies. It was that vision that generated Detroit's implementation struggles. At the same time Canon matched Xerox in the global market in reprographics, despite starting with nothing.

What each Japanese example demonstrates is the power of inspired vision. Moreover, the success of such visions required people at all levels of their companies to share some exciting and creative forces that significantly affected them personally as well as their organizations. Vision focused the energy of thousands of diverse people to generate a common bond and loyalty.

THE NEED FOR VISION

To determine an organization's need for vision it is helpful to pause and think about the following:

- Does the organization have a clear vision statement?

- Do key executives and staff understand the vision?

- Is there a need to take command of the organization's future?

- Do key people or managers disagree over the organization's purpose and mission?

- Do key executives use the vision statement to guide decisions that affect products, markets, and customers?

- Do the organization's people really care about what they are doing?

- Do people assume that current successes guarantee the organization's future?

- Has the organization lost its unique and distinctive reputation? Its pride and commitment? Its interest in risk-taking, new projects, and change?

- Does the organization face significant operational issues that require solutions?

- Does information indicate that the organization is not keeping up with changes in the external environment?

- Does the organization need to develop or rethink its vision in the face of new and unanticipated technological advances or socioeconomic and political changes?

If your responses signal problems, then the time has arrived to create a new direction for the organization.

FORCES PUT IN MOTION

The right shared vision provides an inspiring picture of an ideal destination shared by everyone. It is the force that drives everything in an organization.

The following is a list of some of the key forces that creating and activating the right shared vision can activate:

- Workers' aspirations are elevated as work takes on greater meaning. People want work they can believe in and that has meaning.

- Increased commitment, motivation, excitement, and energy among the people is directed at a common purpose.

- Workers and their jobs are connected by a common aspiration and purpose. Without a shared vision, any organization easily becomes factionalized.

- People become aware of the competencies that distinguish the organization, what it stands for, and where it is headed.

- Activities directly reflect what the organization wants to create. Shared vision provides a context within which workers at all levels can make decisions.

- Risk-taking, creativity, innovation, and experimentation in the organization are promoted.

- A measure is provided that the people can use to evaluate both their worth and the organization's value to society.

By putting such forces into action, the right shared vision provides an inspiring picture of an ideal destination shared by everyone—from top to bottom. Vision provides the foundation for extraordinary human efforts; the framework for strategic and operational decisions; organizational cohesion and teamwork; and an organizational foundation to continue beyond dependence on key people. It is the force that drives everything in an organization. Shared vision arouses in the workers a sense of the uniqueness of their contribution. It empowers everyone to prioritize the work. Creating and integrating a shared vision is one of the most important investments any organization can make. Since such an ideal should always be just beyond reach, it keeps the organization energized and moving.

CHAPTER 4

Where Do You Begin?

FOR MANY LEADERS, a shared vision begins as a personal vision, a dream, a stroke of genius, or simply a "gut feeling." For others it is born of either a combination of intuition and unique insight based on instinct, knowledge, experience, judgment, and imagination, or is a continuous and often chaotic process. These images, impressions, sensations, or dreams become real, however, only with a more concrete expression.

THE QUEST

An organization must undertake a quest to articulate and implement a powerful and easily understood shared vision that will:

- Identify opportunities not seen by other organizations.

- Exploit opportunities that other organizations cannot.

- Be future-oriented and ambitious.

- Reflect the organization's uniqueness accurately.

- Improve job satisfaction.

"Every now and then, a man's mind is stretched by a new idea or sensation, and never shrinks back to its former dimensions."

—Oliver Wendell Holmes, Sr.

19

- Set high standards for productivity and quality.

- Generate enthusiasm, commitment, pride, and loyalty.

- Clarify the new direction by defining what the organization needs to make happen.

AN EFFECTIVE START

The process does not

begin in a vacuum.

An effective start toward building a clear, focused, and shared vision requires careful thought and action. Moreover, despite the absence of precise formulas for finding your vision, the process is much less mystical than we might assume and does not begin in a vacuum. The following steps demystify this process and clarify how to begin.

1. Learn. Learn all you can about the organization, including the business or industry it is in, its past and present vision, purpose or mission, strategy, structure, values, culture, strengths, weaknesses, uniqueness, and what it needs to be successful. Every step in the creation of a promising vision and future must be based on a clear understanding of the present. Identify and consider current business realities as the vision begins to take shape.

2. Think about tomorrow. Start thinking about tomorrow and future business developments. Focus on potential changes in markets and products, key stakeholders and constituencies, and the economic, social, technical, and political environments.

3. Who must buy in? Identify all of the individuals or groups that you want to have a stake—today and tomorrow—in the results of a shared vision. They should include the board of directors, investors, staff, customers, suppliers, and community representatives. The organization's ability to attract and enlist these groups depends on what is known and can be learned about their special interests, goals, needs, and dreams.

4. What is the target? Identify the target of the shared vision. Give careful consideration to:

- What the organization should be doing.

- What the organization must achieve.

- What critical issues the vision must address.

It is important to keep in mind the significance of identifying the target.

5. Focus on success. Focus on the essence of success. One of the essential requirements facing management in the decade ahead is to concentrate less on incremental processes and more on grand results. Every member of the organization must feel they are part of an effort that no other organization has the capability to achieve.

6. Resources. Be prepared to invest resources in your shared vision. For example, where you put key people, money, facilities, and staff directly impacts the success or failure of your vision.

7. Top-down? Abandon the belief that all visions are top-down statements that spring from a charismatic leader possessing mystical or transcendent visionary abilities, or from an organization's planning staff and process.

CHAPTER 5

What Roles Do People Play?

IN CONTRAST TO the hierarchical models of top-down strategy development that most executives practice, the creation of a shared vision provides an organization with significant opportunities for collective action and synergy. Equally as important as the origin and expression of a truly shared vision is the multilevel participation involved in its development and implementation.

In the traditional hierarchical organization, everyone knows that vision and strategy come from the top. Such organizations dismiss the need for sharing or process, assuming that the people have little reason to understand the vision, that all they really need to know is what the organization expects of them. The results of these top-down visions wordsmithed by a PR department or contractor are often disappointing. A major disadvantage of a top-down vision is that, while it may be clear, it is rarely shared. Most of the people lack significant involvement and buy-in. These vision statements find their way to the office or break-room wall rather than the hearts and minds of people. Even worse, vision statements often become sources of resistance and cynicism. Since that is clearly not the intent of a shared vision, leadership and participation are critical. It is important to keep in mind

Shared vision provides significant opportunities for collective action and synergy.

21–27

that it is people who make an organization's shared vision happen. Charisma's role in the creation of a shared vision is highly exaggerated. Moreover, committees, task forces, and planning officers are not sources of shared visions. Visions are the expressions of individuals who merge what they most care about with dreams and opportunities to create a new tomorrow.

Crafting and implementing a vision requires organization leaders to set aside the issues on which they claim expert status. While knowledge of the past is their strength, they will find it necessary to debate the future as equals, not judges. Although, renowned for their impatience and results orientation, leaders will face a seemingly endless array of complex issues. They must recognize that creating a shared vision involves exploration and discovery as much as decision making. Their task is to reject the role of a charismatic leader with a vision and build an organization with a shared vision.

ROLES AND RESPONSIBILITIES

Leadership and

participation

are critical.

Roles and responsibilities in a shared vision process can and do differ. Keep the following in mind as you tailor a visioning process:

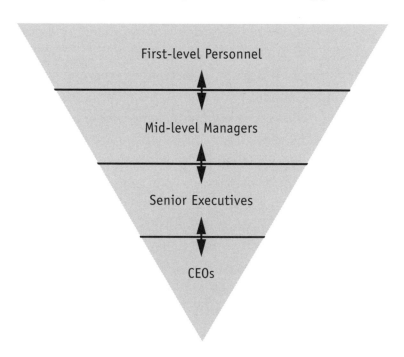

First-level Personnel

Mid-level Managers

Senior Executives

CEOs

24

First-level Personnel

Employees at this level should understand:

- How they will personally benefit from the long-term success of the shared vision.

- How their jobs and priorities are connected to the vision.

Mid-level Managers

As essential participants in the process, with the opportunity to contribute to and critique the vision, their proactive responsibilities include:

- Understanding and explaining the vision and its impact on all aspects of their function.

- Making the vision work through effective communication to staff.

- Providing information to executives regarding critical issues raised by the vision and its implementation.

Senior Executives

As the CEO's alter egos, senior executives:

- Have a key role in developing and articulating a clear and inspiring shared vision that reflects their commitment.

- Are the vision's champions, giving it life by constantly demonstrating their commitment and communicating it.

- Must regularly review all decisions in their areas to make certain they reflect and contribute to the success of the vision.

- Make certain that the shared vision shares equal time with operational needs.

Chief Executive Officers

As the embodiment of a future-focused, shared vision, a CEO's most critical roles and responsibilities include:

- Providing leadership and taking an active role in the creation of a vision and setting a direction so compelling that everyone will follow.

- Being open and willing to listen to and entertain diverse ideas.

- Accepting responsibility as the organization's change agent.

- Being the standard-bearer, cheerleader, and chief negotiator when the vision is articulated internally and externally.

- Becoming mentor and model of the vision for the organization.

- Making certain that strategies and decisions at all levels are consistent with the organization's shared vision.

- Keeping an open mind and planning for periodic adjustments of the vision as critical issues surface and the environment changes.

- Implementing a performance evaluation and reward system based on the shared vision.

At this point, it should be evident that the success of a shared vision hinges on the actions of everyone in an organization. From top to bottom, the daily actions and decisions of the people must reflect and reinforce the vision. Without such a commitment it will ultimately fail.

CHAPTER 6

Getting Where You Want to Go

IT IS A SIGNIFICANT OVERSTATEMENT to say that successful shared visions are always the result of orderly processes. Nevertheless, certain steps can put into order the key elements that organizations find useful in creating a new tomorrow. In the following discussion of these steps, however, keep two factors in mind.

28–31

- First, because building a shared vision is such a creative and introspective experience, some people will be extremely uncomfortable with inherent complexities and ambiguities.

- Second, it is essential to remember that a shared vision is a qualitative assessment of an organization and the present and future environment it faces.

Hard vs. Soft Data.

This means much of the data are *soft*, in contrast to the *hard* data that most planning and analysis processes generate today. While hard data may inform, soft data provide the insights and wisdom that become the foundation of an effective shared vision. In order to acquire such knowledge and apply it effectively to building a shared vision, you must ask the right questions.

The following phases help expose, assemble, and collect the impressions, opinions, and creative thinking needed to move an organization from where it currently is to where it wants to go.

PHASE I: CURRENT ORGANIZATION AUDIT

Building a shared vision starts with a clear understanding of the current composition, operation, and direction of the organization and the fundamentals of the business it is in. To do this, examine the basic elements of the organization, its business, how it operates, its markets, users, its profitability, and its future if it continues on its current path.

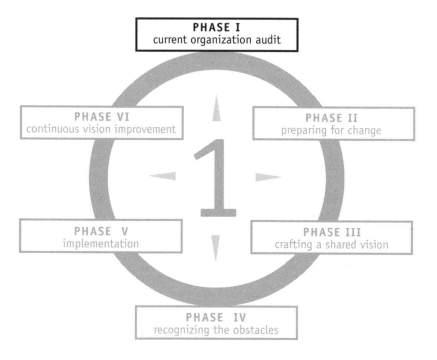

Examples of the questions you need to ask and answer include:

- Does the organization have a vision statement?

- Could you and your key executives/managers write a brief statement of the vision?

- Does the organization have a mission or purpose statement?

- Does the organization have a unique characteristic or competence?

- What are the organization's strengths, weaknesses, and areas of special skill?

- What is the scope of current products, services, markets, and customers?

- Can you identify which current products, services, markets, and customers will be expanded or dropped in the future?

- Are there current plans for new products, services, markets, and customers to be developed and emphasized?

- What distinguishes the organization's products and services from all the others?

- Are the organization's current structures, processes, personnel policies, and information systems adequate?

- Do the organization's key people know and agree on its direction?

- What is the organization's current driving force?

In addition to a picture of the organization in its present state, the answers to these and similar questions provide a focus for responding to all of the threats and opportunities in the external environment. The organization has a framework for vision.

PHASE II: PREPARING FOR CHANGE

Having generated baseline information and determined the organization's need and readiness for a shared vision, the next step is to design it.

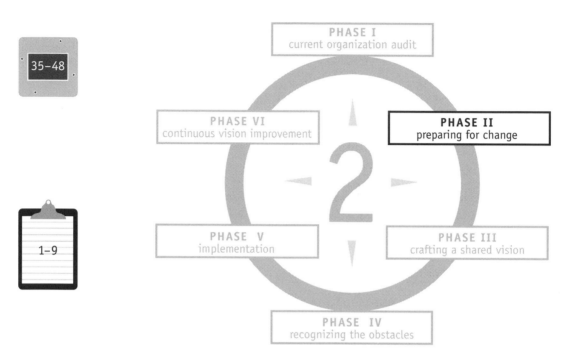

Providing the organization with a vision design that is clear and focused requires thoughtful consideration of the following questions:

What Are the Key Issues?

Each organization has basic issues and concerns that require clarification and total understanding to focus its vision. For example:

- What is the direction of future business development?

- What future range of products, services, and markets will we consider?

- How will the current and future ranges of products, services, and markets differ?

- Will future products, services, and markets be prioritized so the appropriate resources will be focused on the vision?

- What key capabilities and resources will the organization need for the new shared vision to succeed?

- How will the new shared vision affect anticipated growth and return?

- Who must the organization satisfy?

Who Must the Organization Satisfy?

Each organization has internal and external constituencies made up of individuals, groups, or institutions that have a significant stake in its future. Since each constituency has a particular involvement with the organization, it is likely that their interests, priorities, and expectations will differ. At the same time, constituencies can provide critical insights into possible future developments and the vision. More importantly, they exert varying degrees of influence on the vision. Any one of them could present the organization with an opportunity or a challenge. Therefore, in order to understand their roles it is important to know as much as possible about each of them. Start by making a list and ranking the organization's critical constituencies. Finally, make an effort to understand each one's primary interests and expectations about the organization's future.

How Will Everyone Know When They Get There?

From the start of the process it is important to remember that a vision will be battered and tested externally and internally. The complexities and uncertainties of a tumultuous social, political, and economic future are the primary drivers of external challenges. Meanwhile, internally, all members of the organization will find themselves accountable for making decisions and taking actions that must be consistent with the shared vision. What they have created becomes the critical benchmark for measuring performance and evaluation. While that sounds easy to do, people in organizations have experienced surprising difficulty working and being evaluated on the basis of rules that they themselves created and accepted. But, that is precisely what they must do. The implementation of a shared vision commits everyone to a performance evaluation based on criteria they created for themselves.

The implementation of a shared vision commits everyone to a performance evaluation based on criteria they created for themselves.

31

Feedback is essential.

Implementing and sustaining a shared vision in the face of these external and internal realities requires, among other things, a carefully thought-out evaluation process and procedure. Minimally, it should provide the organization with two significant sources of information. First, whatever the process and procedure, the system must keep everyone accurately informed regarding the continued soundness of the information and underlying assumptions on which the shared vision was based. This is especially important because the future never happens exactly as forecasted. Moreover, the procedure must provide information continuously and require it as a permanent agenda item at all vision planning and review sessions.

When designing an evaluation system, it is important to keep the following in mind:

- A key to the successful creation and implementation of a shared vision is the extent of its impact on internal accountability for all decisions and actions.

- From a list of assumptions and categories, identify and prioritize the key points that will determine if the vision is on or off target.

- The organization should have ways to determine whether it is working with customers/users and suppliers as the shared vision clearly states.

- People should have ways to determine whether they are working with each other in ways that are congruent with the shared vision.

- All senior executives should have valid and useful data telling them how they and their direct reports are doing.

- The organization should provide everyone with valid and consistent information that clearly shows how well they and the organization are doing.

- Shared vision review and evaluation sessions should be routinely scheduled.

Will There Be Limitations?

For a vision to clearly express the organization's new direction it should state what will or will not be included. Depending on its business or industry, certain time frames, geographical restraints, socioeconomic and financial realities, as well as the future political environment should be considered carefully in every stage of vision creation.

For example, the issue of how far into the future the vision should focus will be influenced by the changes to be made and the estimated time needed to implement them. How important is it, if at all, to have a specific time frame in mind in the creation of your vision? Although there is no definitive answer to the question, if a time length is established, keep in mind that with achievement comes the necessity for revision or recreation. Geographic restraints, on the other hand, will be determined by such factors as fixed boundaries, legal and license requirements, regulatory agencies, and marketing to specific customers or users.

How Do You Control the Competitive Arena?

One of the marks of an effective shared vision is the extent to which it reflects the organization's recognition that it is important to influence, if not control, the competitive arena. This can be a difficult task in view of the fact that competition has changed, intensified, and become more complex. In general, competition has become increasingly difficult to anticipate, track, comprehend, and combat. In addition, the definition of competition has been expanded beyond the traditional or identifiable competitors to include any person, organization, or movement that reduces or eliminates customers.

Competition has changed.

The solution lies in responding to competition with a proactive, rather than reactive, shared vision. Here are some suggestions on how to do this:

Be proactive.

- Identify all real or potential changes in the competition.

- Develop a scenario for each competitor that anticipates their response and strategy in terms of products, customers, and geographic markets to the new shared vision.

- Using this knowledge of the competition's strategy, develop a plan to manage it.

How Do You Become a Futurist?

Visions must deal with the future.

Many organizations use an assortment of tools that lead them to think they can see into the future: market research, scenario planning, forecasting technology, competitor analysis, and others. Despite the usefulness of these tools, by themselves, they cannot produce a shared vision. They all fail to drive leaders to seriously consider reconceiving the organization and its competitive arena. It is only when leaders do this, and in doing so become futurists, that they can begin creating the future.

Since visions are statements of what the organization will create in the years ahead, leaders must deal with the future. Of course, that requires the organization and its leaders to develop the ability to think long-term. Although some leaders see themselves as their organization's only futurist, others choose to create and lead research teams to study future developments and potential changes that can affect the organization.

Creating a vision requires taking a stand for a preferred future.

By becoming futurists, leaders find it easier to project their thinking about a range of possible futures for the organization in a systematic way. In turn, this stimulates them and others to develop a greater range of possible visions from which they can jointly select the best.

Here are a few questions that can serve as catalysts in clarifying the future and developing a shared vision:

- If you could create the future, what future would you create for your organization?

- How many categories of future developments can you currently identify that you believe will influence the organization and the shared vision statement?

- Can you make a list of expectations, based on the time frame of the shared vision statement, for each of the above categories?

- Can you prioritize a list of those expectations that would have the greatest impact on the shared vision statement?

PHASE III: CRAFTING A SHARED VISION

The time has come to put it all together—intuition, personal visions, experience, judgment, information, values, and culture—to create the shared vision that will distinguish your organization from all the other look-alikes. To do this it must be distinctive and establish standards that others will find difficult, but necessary to follow. How do you do this? In crafting a vision, consider the following as a helpful model.

Put it all together to create the shared vision that will distinguish your organization from all the other look-alikes.

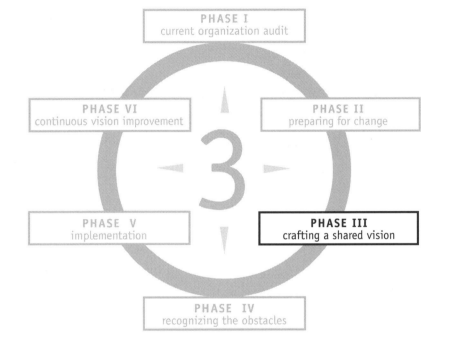

Step One: Knowledge Is Important

Start by reviewing all the information and materials that have been compiled. In doing this, however, keep in mind that a significant source of this knowledge about the organization and its industry/business is based on direct experience. From that experience leaders have gained valuable information about what happens, how things happen, and who makes things happen in the organization.

That knowledge then becomes the source for much of the insight that goes into crafting an attractive shared vision. It is important at this early stage to stay flexible and receptive to ideas, intuition, and

Stay flexible and receptive.

unique insights, regardless of the source. Look for lots of ideas in places you may have been avoiding.

Step Two: The Driving Force

Behind each organization or business is a particular force, element, or motive that distinguishes it from all other organizations and gives it a special identity. The identification of what now drives the organization and has pushed it in its current direction can be a key factor in considering future directions and shared visions.

It is especially important for an organization to know its driving force if it is likely to change direction as a result of visioning. The driving force plays a significant role in determining the organization's future and its shared vision.

Although as many as ten variables or areas may influence an organization, only one emerges as the primary source of its driving force. The following is a list of representative key areas from which an organization should be able to identify its driving force:

Potential Driving Forces

- Products or service offered
- Users/customers
- Markets served
- Low-cost production, capability/capacity
- Marketing/sales methods
- Technology
- Method of distribution
- Return/profit
- Size/growth
- Natural resources

Behind each organization is a particular force that distinguishes it and gives it a special identity.

Step Three: Rank the Options

The next step is to develop a list of prioritized and tested shared visions that can produce success for the organization and its major constituent groups. Prioritize the list of visions with the chief criteria being the most attractive and promising. When you complete the ranking, start at the top and test each one against the desired elements of a successful vision and other success factors that have been discussed. Finally, determine whether the elements are consistent with the organization's strengths, driving force, culture, and values. Is this important or is change a higher priority?

Step Four: Choose the Best

Finally, choose and state, as clearly as possible, the best vision from the prioritized list of possible alternatives. Put the vision on paper. This forces everyone to think again about what exactly they are attempting to do. Moreover, it is a significant step toward making it a shared vision, rather than the vision of a single leader. Keep in mind, however, that although intuition and experience may make the choice seem obvious, it is important to test again against the key elements of a vision discussed earlier.

Vision focus. Once you are satisfied that this is the vision the organization really wants, put it into a short, easily understood statement that focuses on:

- An exciting future.

- Creating value for others.

- Market advantage factors that set standards of excellence and reflect the high ideals, standards, and uniqueness of the organization to everyone who interacts with it.

- Providing clear decision-making criteria.

- Inspiring enthusiasm and commitment.

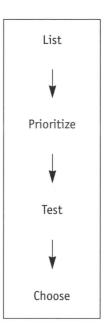

PHASE IV: RECOGNIZING THE OBSTACLES

The process of information collection, analysis, and judgment has led the organization to choose a new direction. At this point it would be wise to stop and reflect on the new vision by asking:

57–64

- Is this the best vision?

- What are the chances for its success?

- If it fails, what can be salvaged?

- Should we even try?

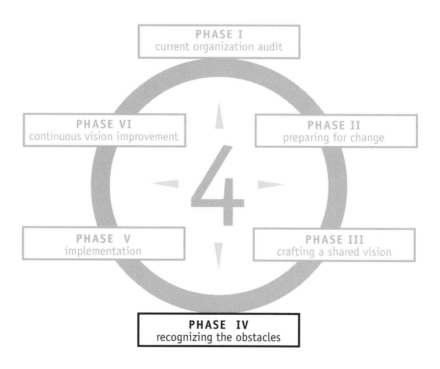

Do the Leaders Believe in the Vision?

Doubt and uncertainty are potential, even inevitable, when an organization embarks in a new direction.

It is important to ask questions in order to remove any doubts that the new vision inspires commitment and enthusiasm—especially that of the leaders. Does management really believe in this vision? Before you can ask others to commit, you must totally convince them that the vision is right for the organization's internal and external environment. Is it right for everyone who will interact with it, and will it lead to improved performance?

Exercises for recognizing the obstacles. Answers to the following questions could be provided by conducting a series of meetings, focus groups or surveys with employees at all levels of the organization. By answering these questions the organization will have provided itself with a test of the vision.

- Is it clearly understood?

- How does it compare with the "old"?

- What is its effect (impact) on the organization and was this anticipated?
    - Barriers and critical issues
    - Business and production processes to be changed
    - New training needs
    - List critical issues now facing the organization

- What is its effect on the competition and was this anticipated?

Is the Vision Clearly Understood?

Be certain that everyone who will implement and live with the new vision clearly understands it. People commit to a vision only when they fully understand it. Although there are many ways to test for understanding of the vision, here are three effective and commonly used methods.

Understanding is a critical step toward commitment.

1. Use a small group of people whose views you value and with whom you feel comfortable and can trust to be honest as a sounding board.
2. Find ways to meet and talk informally and in relaxed conditions with employees, managers, colleagues, customers, and suppliers about their understanding of the vision. Internally, make every effort to hear from a cross-section of functions and organizational levels.

3. There are formal ways to test the impact and understanding of the vision. Printed materials, such as memos, newsletters, and bulletin board displays are very popular. In addition, you should make the time for and develop the skill to conduct general employee meetings. These offer an excellent way to develop understanding and commitment.

Have You Compared the Old and New?

Take the time to give careful thought to comparing the new vision to the organization's current vision, mission, or purpose. The questions that need to be considered include:

Remember where

the organization

has been.

- How far apart are the two visions?

- What changes, if any, will be required to make the transition to new products, markets, and customers?

- Will the new vision require new resources, suppliers, and skills?

- Is the time frame for its achievement realistic?

- Based on the answers to these and related questions, does the new vision need modification?

How Will the New Vision Affect the Organization?

Answering this fourth question involves another important comparison. It identifies any differences or similarities between the new vision and the information in the current organization audit, which focuses

What are its chances

of success?

on the internal and external environments. For example:

- Does the new vision maximize the organization's particular strengths and conversely, minimize its weakness?

- Does the new vision challenge the organization's current culture?

- How well does the new vision respond to the organization's current and future opportunities and threats?

How Will the New Vision Affect the Competition?

Answering the final question can determine which, if any, competing organizations will be attracted to the new vision. Of course, if the new vision reflects a change it will naturally attract new competitors. More importantly, ask if the new shared vision will enable the organization to control or influence the competitive arena and the new competitor's strategy as it had those in the past? Thinking about the following will bring these concerns into sharper focus:

Will the new shared vision enable the organization to control or influence the competitive arena?

- Does the new vision challenge the competition's strengths and exploit their weaknesses?

- What do you think the competition's reactions will be to the new vision, and can their actions be neutralized?

- What is each competitor's strategy or vision and what is driving it?

- Does the new vision counteract each competitor's particular expertise and competence?

The questions and answers in this step reveal some critical issues that require attention and resolution if the shared vision is to become a reality. The issues, when resolved, provide a bridge between the old and new vision. Once you are satisfied with the answers, your organization's new vision is ready for implementation.

Phase V: Implementation—Vision in Action

The new vision is nothing more than a statement until it is widely shared, accepted, and put into action. While the words are very important, it is only after the vision is put into action that it acquires the power to change an organization and move it in a new direction.

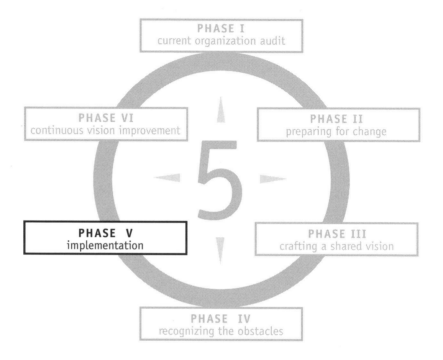

Action and Commitment

Putting a new vision into action presents an organization with the same challenges commonly associated with implementing any significant organizational change. It requires similar action and commitment. Action gives life to the new vision. Commitment inspires people to buy into a vision and understand what it means for them personally. As is the case with any major attempt at change, the actions needed to implement a vision demand quality communication among all levels of the organization. These actions also require that leaders, openly and consistently, give top priority to the allocation of time and resources needed to support the new vision.

Internal Tools

If the vision is to become a reality, people must commit to using it. To inspire people at all levels to commit to using the vision, you need to persuade them to change their perceptions of what is important for them and the organization. Here are some useful considerations:

1. It is critical that the chief executive and senior management openly demonstrate their personal commitment to the new vision by their actions. They must accept the roles of direction setters, change agents, communicators, and coaches. As visionary leaders they must consistently apply the vision to all of their actions and decisions and look for opportunities to communicate it. Their purpose is to get the message across that using the shared vision is the thing to do.

   Keep in mind that communicating the vision to the organization or to a group or unit can present a challenge. In a complex or growing organization, helping people comprehend the most recent plan and their role in its implementation can be a major task. But, attempting to get everyone to understand a vision of a new future presents a communication problem that is significantly greater in scope. Therefore, it is vital that the vision be communicated in words that are clear, vivid, engaging, and that arouse emotion and excitement.

2. From the start, management at all levels must commit to communicating the vision to everyone. People need to know that the vision is working. Everyone must be constantly reminded that the success of the vision will propel the organization to the top in its industry or business. On a personal level, employees need to know the level of commitment that management has made to the success of the vision. In addition, leaders must regularly announce and demonstrate the opportunities that applying the vision holds for each member of the organization.

> If the vision is to become reality, people must use it.

> People need to know that the vision is working.

If the actions and words of

the management team fail

to reinforce the vision it

is doomed.

3. While the leader of an organization is the primary communicator of the vision, the vision is doomed if the actions and words of the management team fail to reinforce it. From the beginning, leaders must personally and directly involve those reporting to them. Senior executives must be enthusiastically committed to the vision. The next step involves getting a similar commitment from the entire management and supervisory staff. Coaching and supporting roles must rise to the top of every manager's responsibilities. Rather than giving lip service to such terms as *participative management* and *empowerment*, it is essential they apply them. The organization's managers must recognize that they have key roles and are accountable in the implementation of the new shared vision. People will naturally turn to their immediate managers when looking for a role model as they begin applying the new vision.

4. Organization leaders have access to powerful internal management tools and systems they can use to communicate and reinforce their personal commitment to a new shared vision. The three most effective tools or systems that get the attention of people in an organization include performance appraisal, personnel policies, and culture.

Performance appraisal system. A performance appraisal system clarifies what the leadership expects. The performance appraisal system plays an important role in vision implementation. It puts people on notice that they are expected to use, specifically and quantifiably, the new vision, and that there will be evaluation, feedback, and reward.

Personnel policies. Reward is provided by the personnel system. Policies can provide useful complementary mechanisms to keep the shared vision uppermost in people's minds. Such policies include recruitment, employee orientation, training, and compensation guidelines.

Culture. Finally, the organization's culture, or values, identifies what is right and provides an almost changeless sense of purpose and reason for existence that goes well beyond simply making a profit. Both for individuals and corporatewide, the culture is a primary source of motivation. Priorities, strategies, or goals that fail to reflect the culture or values are vulnerable to procrastination, compromise, or abandonment. Its culture drives and empowers the organization toward accomplishment of the vision. This commitment to culture or ideology has freed many organizations to change, improve, or renew everything else in the development and implementation of a successful vision. As important as appraisal systems and personnel policies are, commitment to the new shared vision is significantly enhanced when it is shaped or reshaped to preserve the organization's culture and core values. To accomplish this requires the use of an assortment of activities, rewards, team building, orientation programs, and employee training based on the shared vision to build an organization climate that complements it.

Use the tools together. At this point, as plans for putting the new vision into action are formulated, it is important to remember that excessive reliance on any one of these strategies jeopardizes the successful launching of the new vision. Despite the significant contributions of communication, performance appraisal systems, personnel policies, and organizational culture in mobilizing people, the shared vision and potential changes will fall short of the desired goal if any one of them is applied in isolation. They make a significant difference only when combined and integrated in support of action and commitment to the new vision and direction.

Making It Happen

With commitment from the top and policy tools established to support the vision, an implementation plan for launching the vision can be made. This plan will include work sessions at all levels of the organization to determine how the vision will change the objectives and goals of each work unit. Mechanisms for monitoring the effect of the vision will also be established. Refer to Parts 2, 3, and 4 for the support tools to help you implement the five phases of this organizational visioning method.

PHASE VI: CONTINUOUS VISION IMPROVEMENT

Does the vision statement

still have meaning in

the organization?

To keep the new shared vision alive over a period of time requires periodic reviews and updates. These reevaluations and commitment renewals provide a vital check on the progress of vision implementation. Does the vision statement still have meaning in the organization? Do the assumptions and judgments from which the new vision sprang remain valid?

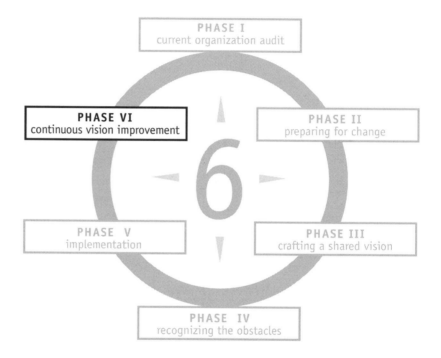

In addition, since vision is, by definition, always just beyond reach, you must continuously refine and revise it to cope with critical issues generated by ongoing changes in the organization's internal and external environments. As long as the shared vision can stay ahead of the rapidly changing times, it needs reaffirmation and support.

Although no set rules say when to reevaluate the vision, it is usually done within six to twelve months of implementation. At this time, focus on the impact of changes in the internal and external environments and the monitoring of progress made on critical issues. After that, review the vision regularly or as environmental factors appear that threaten its success. Keep in mind that vision crafting provides an excellent agenda for the review of potential changes in the vision. The new vision must keep the organization and its people on the cutting edge of growth.

The new vision must keep

the organization and its

people on the cutting

edge of growth.

Summary

LOOKING BACK at the key points about what a shared vision is and how an organization can make it happen covers the following:

- Visioning is the starting point for total quality management, process improvement, process management, continuous improvement, and reengineering.

- A thoughtfully created and implemented vision sustains an organization's commitment to change through the process of change.

- In today's economy leaders must ask more than just how we can redeploy assets and rethink operational strategy in response to our competitive environment. Far more critical questions focus on what we want to create.

- A shared vision is a statement that captures an ideal, unique, and attractive image of an organization's future and answers the question, What do we want to create?

- In addition to identifying and defining the new tomorrow—a mutual destination—a shared vision provides the framework that guides all decision making, planning, and action.

- Visioning is much more than a powerful tool—it is a strategy, culture, and mental attitude for expanding the organization's horizons about what can be.

- A shared vision provides an inspiring picture of an ideal destination that everyone, from top to bottom, shares. Since such an ideal should always be just beyond reach, it keeps the organization energized and moving.

- For many leaders, a shared vision begins as a personal vision, a dream, a stroke of genius, or simply a "gut feeling." For others, it is born of either a combination of intuition and unique insight, or a continuous and often chaotic process.

- In contrast to the hierarchical models of top-down strategy development that most executives practice, the creation of a shared vision provides an organization with significant opportunities for collective action and synergy.

- While hard data may inform, it is "soft" data that provides the insights and wisdom on which to build an effective shared vision.

- Building a shared vision starts with a clear understanding of the current composition, operation, and direction of the organization and the fundamentals of the business it is in.

- All organizations have basic issues and concerns that require clarification and total understanding for its vision to be focused.

- The crafting of a shared vision that distinguishes your organization from other look-alikes is the sum of intuition, personal visions, experiences, judgment, information, values, and culture.

- Throughout the visioning process, pause and answer questions to remove any doubts that the new vision inspires commitment and enthusiasm.

- While the words are very important, it is only after the vision is put into action that it acquires the power to change an organization and move it in a new direction.

- To keep the new shared vision alive over a period of time requires periodic reviews and updates.

- The new vision must keep the organization and its people on the cutting edge of growth.

PART II

METHODOLOGY FOR VISION DEVELOPMENT

Six Phases to Success

SIX PHASES OF VISION DEVELOPMENT are presented in Part II. Charts summarize the steps, activities, and support tools that are necessary to develop and implement a shared vision. It is important to keep in mind that these activities provide one of the most powerful ways of producing a shared vision.

FACILITATION

It should be noted that as the organization begins this work it is important to identify and appoint a knowledgeable and trained facilitator. Although as critical as this position is to the success of the organization's effort, an internal or external appointment is a matter of choice. In addition to implementing and coordinating the activities discussed and outlined in Part II, the facilitator's responsibilities include:

- Helping the leaders scope and structure the organization's process and deliverables that create an effective shared vision.

- Planning, preparing, and providing documentation of all the sessions and related data.

- Possessing the skills and knowledge that will help produce all the elements needed to craft a shared vision.

- Challenging the status quo.

- Creating a climate that views obstacles as opportunities.

- Providing clear and timely feedback.

- Constantly reminding the organization that it's not what it is today, but what you want it to be tomorrow.

- Asking questions that produce actions and solutions to problems.

- Utilizing techniques that generate the broadest participation in the decision making that produces a shared vision.

METHODOLOGY OVERVIEW

Phase I: Current Organization Audit

In the first phase of organization vision development the chief executives and senior management determine an approach that best suits the organization's needs. After finalizing a plan that outlines the project scope and timeline, the assessment instruments should be customized to gather information about the organization and its competitors. A session should then be conducted to introduce the personnel of the organization to the concept and process of organizational visioning. In addition, the assessments should be distributed, completed, and analyzed.

Phase II: Preparing for Change

The organization must now go through the process of assessment and development of an Organizational Vision. This begins with the use of information gathered in Phase I to clarify the current profiles of the organization and its competitors. In this phase the essential Organizational Vision design factors will be examined in preparation for choosing and crafting a vision.

Phase III: Crafting a Shared Vision

The result of this phase will be the crafting and refinement of an Organizational Vision. Included will be an examination of the organization's primary driving element or force, and the internal and external organization variables that appear most likely to have future impact. The organization will draft a vision statement and perform a series of exercises designed to evaluate and refine the new vision.

Phase IV: Recognizing the Obstacles

The organization must now analyze the internal and external impact of the Organizational Vision. Included in this phase will be an examination of business and production process changes, training needs, and competitor's reactions to the vision. The outcome of this phase will be the identification of all current critical issues that will need to be resolved.

Phase V: Implementation—Vision in Action

Making Vision Happen. During this phase, the migration by the organization toward the new Organizational Vision will begin. The first step will be the generation of a blueprint that will guide implementation. The blueprint prioritizes changes in business and production processes, macro-level training needs requiring attention, and critical issues to resolve. Plans to revise processes and meet training needs will be initiated.

Keeping Vision a Vital Force. Implementation work sessions at all levels of the organization are now conducted. During this phase the organization must monitor the effects of the vision on decision-making, planning, production processes, organization policies and procedures, and training. Implementation work sessions may be conducted for a year or more before the effects of vision have been understood well enough to move to the final phase of improving the vision.

Phase VI: Continuous Vision Improvement

The final phase of the Organizational Vision process involves evaluation and refinement. This is based on the performance evaluation of the Organizational Vision over a specified period of time—often at the end of the first year of implementation. Particular attention will be focused on the identification and prioritization of new or continuing critical issues that need to be solved.

PHASE I

Current Organization Audit

In the first phase of organization vision development the chief executives and senior management determine an approach that best suits the organization's needs. After finalizing a plan that outlines the project scope and timeline, the assessment instruments should be customized to gather information about the organization and its competitors.

A session should then be conducted to introduce the personnel of the organization to the concept and process of organizational visioning. In addition, the assessments should be distributed, completed, and analyzed.

The steps, activities, and support tools for this phase are listed in the table below.

STEPS	ACTIVITIES	SUPPORT TOOLS
1. Plan the visioning program	• Conduct CEO interview • Determine scope, purpose, • participants, basic timeline • Develop detailed program, project timeline	Assessment No. 1
2. Customize the surveys	• Organization Vision Assessment • Vision Needs Assessment • Current Organization Profile • Strategic Profile Assessment • Competitors Assessment	Assessment No. 3 Assessment No. 3 Assessment No. 4 Assessment No. 5 Assessment No. 6 Assessment Nos. 7–9
3. Conduct Session I	• Review program and project timeline • What is vision? • Why do it? • Where to begin? • Key roles people play • Key elements	Overhead Nos. 1-34
4. Distribute and complete the surveys	• Interview senior executives • Organization Vision Assessment • Vision Needs Assessment • Current Organization Profile	Assessment No. 2 Assessment No. 3 Assessment No. 4 Assessment No. 5
5. Analyze the information	• Compile results of interviews and assessments and write summary reports	Assessment Nos. 1–5
6. Distribute and complete the competitor surveys	• Competitor Assessment: Key Questions • Competitor Assessment • Competitor Information Sources	Assessment Nos. 7–9

<table>
<tr><td rowspan="5">

PHASE II

**Preparing
for
Change**
</td></tr>
</table>

The organization must now go through the process of assessment and development of an Organizational Vision. This begins with the use of information gathered in Phase I to clarify the current profiles of the organization and its competitors. In this phase the essential Organizational Vision design factors will be examined in preparation for choosing and crafting a vision.

The steps, activities, and support tools for this phase are listed in the table below.

STEPS	ACTIVITIES	SUPPORT TOOLS
1. Conduct Session II	• Discuss results of CEO and senior management interviews • Discuss results of Organization Vision Assessment, Vision Needs Assessment, Current Organization Profile • Introduce preparing for change factors • Develop a list of key issues	Assessment Nos. 1-2 Assessment Nos. 3-5 Overhead Nos. 35-48
2. Analyze constituencies	• List • Prioritize • Identify interests and expectations	
3. Establish an evaluation process	• Identify criteria for creation or modification of procedure • Identify and agree on vision limitations or parameters	
4. Analyze the information	• Compile the results of the competitors assessment and write a report • Develop a proactive plan to manage competition	Assessment Nos. 7-9
5. Become a futurist	• Determine the future developments that will influence the organization • List and rank in order of importance the expectations that will impact the vision statement	Overhead Nos. 46-48
6. Distribute Strategic Profile Assessment	• Strategic Profile Assessment	Assessment No. 6

PHASE III

Crafting a Shared Vision

The result of this phase will be the crafting and refinement of an Organizational Vision. Included will be an examination of the organization's primary driving element or force, and the internal and external organization variables that appear most likely to have future impact. The organization will draft a vision statement and perform a series of exercises designed to evaluate and refine the new vision.

The steps, activities, and support tools for this phase are listed in the table below.

STEPS	ACTIVITIES	SUPPORT TOOLS
1. Analyze strategic profile	• Collect Strategic Profile Assessment • Compile data from Strategic Profile Assessment and write a summary report	Assessment No. 6
2. Conduct Session III	• Discuss Strategic Profile Assessment data • Reach consensus on organization driving force or logic • List and prioritize possible visions • Test or evaluate prioritized visions • Identify and agree on vision that best meets criteria • Write vision statement	Overhead Nos. 49–56
3. Test the vision	• Review steps for testing the vision • Distribute exercises and activities to be completed for testing the vision	

PHASE IV

Recognizing the Obstacles

The organization must now analyze the internal and external impact of the Organizational Vision. Included in this phase will be an examination of business and production process changes, training needs, and competitors reactions to the vision. The outcome of this phase will be the identification of all current critical issues that will need to be resolved.

The steps, activities, and support tools for this phase are listed in the table below.

STEPS	ACTIVITIES	SUPPORT TOOLS
1. Testing the vision	• Collect Recognizing the Obstacles exercises • Compile and summarize the exercise results	(see page 39)
2. Conduct Session IV	• Review results of Recognizing the Obstacles exercises and activities • Is the vision understood? • Compare old and new visions • Assess effect on organization • Identify barriers and critical issues to be solved • Identify and prioritize business and production processes to be changed • Identify and prioritize macro-level training needs • Assess and prioritize effect on competition • List and prioritize critical issues	Overhead Nos. 57–64

<table>
<tr><td>

PHASE V

Implementation —Vision in Action

</td><td>

Making Vision Happen

During this phase the migration by the organization toward the new Organizational Vision will begin. The first step will be the generation of a blueprint that will guide implementation. The blueprint prioritizes changes in business and production processes, macro-level training needs requiring attention, and critical issues to resolve. Plans to revise processes and meet training needs will be initiated.

</td></tr>
</table>

Keeping Vision a Vital Force

Implementation work sessions at all levels of the organization are now conducted. During this phase, the organization must monitor the effects of the vision on decision-making, planning, production processes, organization policies and procedures, and training.

Implementation work sessions may be conducted for a year or more before the effects of the vision have been understood well enough to move to the final phase of improving the vision.

The steps, activities, and support tools for this phase are listed in the table below.

STEPS	ACTIVITIES	SUPPORT TOOLS
1. Commitment	• Gain CEO and senior executive commitment • Develop blueprint for implementation	
2. Conduct Session V	• Communicate the vision • Present blueprint for implementation	Overhead Nos. 65–72
3. Plan	• Develop plan to revise business and production processes • Develop plan to meet macro-level training needs	
4. Work sessions	• Arrange and begin implementation work sessions with all work units • Identify all new critical issues as they arise	
5. Revitalizing the vision	• Periodically schedule organization unit, vision implementation, work and progress sessions • Identify and prioritize all new critical issues as they arise	

PHASE VI
Continuous Vision Improvement

The final phase of the Organizational Vision process involves evaluation and refinement. This is based on the performance evaluation of the Organizational Vision over a specified period of time—often at the end of the first year of implementation. Particular attention will be focused on the identification and prioritization of new or continuing critical issues that need to be solved.

The steps, activities, and support tools for this phase are listed in the table below.

STEPS	ACTIVITIES	SUPPORT TOOLS
1. Conduct Session VI	• Conduct group work sessions • Review the steps for crafing the vision • Review new and updated critical issues • Refine or revise the vision as necessary	Overhead Nos. 73–74
2. Refine or revise the vision	• As needed, repeat the cycle of phases to keep the vision vital and relevant to the current organization profile	

PART III

ORGANIZATIONAL VISIONING ASSESSMENTS

Nine Tools for Testing

THE FOLLOWING ASSESSMENT TOOLS have been created to help an organization or unit to identify the organization's visioning needs and opportunities, as well as to perform a current condition analysis. The assessments, depending on the target, can be answered during personal interviews or in groups. The result should be the gathering of soft and hard data, anecdotal information, and the benchmarking of significant competitors.

Chief Executive Officer Assessment

Organization: _____

1. What is the purpose of this organization?

   _____

   _____

2. Does your organization have a vision (strategy) statement?

   ☐ Yes   ☐ No   ☐ Not sure

3. Can you write a brief statement that summarizes the organization vision?

   ☐ Yes   ☐ No   ☐ Not sure

4. Is the vision statement formally communicated to everyone in the organization?

   ☐ Yes   ☐ No   ☐ Not sure

5. Is the vision statement clearly understood at all levels of the organization?

   ☐ Yes   ☐ No   ☐ Not sure

6. Is your vision statement clearly understood by your direct reports and senior management/administrative staff?

   ☐ Yes   ☐ No   ☐ Not sure

7. Can your direct reports write a brief statement (without assistance) that summarizes the organization's vision?

   ☐ Yes   ☐ No   ☐ Not sure

8. Do you find your organization's vision statement helpful when making decisions about products, services, customers, users, or markets?

   ☐ Yes   ☐ No   ☐ Not sure

9. Do your direct reports and senior management/administrative staff refer to the vision statement when making decisions about products, services, customers, users, or markets?

   ☐ Yes   ☐ No   ☐ Not sure

10. Are you satisfied with the amount of time you have committed to empower people in the organization to use the vision statement?

    ☐ Yes   ☐ No   ☐ Not sure

11. What are the three (3) most significant problems facing the organization right now?

_____

_____

_____

12. Does the organization's vision statement help to solve these problems?

☐ Yes ☐ No ☐ Not sure

13. Is the current vision statement the result of an attempt by you and your direct reports to reach consensus on the future direction of the organization?

☐ Yes ☐ No ☐ Not sure

14. Are you satisfied that the organization's vision statement was reached by consensus with your direct reports?

☐ Yes ☐ No ☐ Not sure

15. Does the organization's vision have internal critics?

☐ Yes ☐ No ☐ Not sure

16. Do you know where (departments, job categories, employee types, geographic locations, etc.) the key critics are located?

☐ Yes ☐ No ☐ Not sure

17. In your opinion, is the location/distribution of the key vision critics directly related to what is bothering them?

☐ Yes ☐ No ☐ Not sure

18. Does the organization offer training to employees at all levels, in the use and/or application of the vision to their work?

☐ Yes ☐ No ☐ Not sure

19. In your opinion, is all training, internal and external, related to the use and/or application of the organization's vision?

☐ Yes ☐ No ☐ Not sure

20. Does the organization include an evaluation of the use and/or application of the vision in performance appraisals?

☐ Yes ☐ No ☐ Not sure

ORGANIZATIONAL VISIONING   **1**

---

21. Does your organization utilize a separate process to determine *what* it wants to become (i.e., visioning) as opposed to a process that determines *how* to get there (i.e., strategic planning)?

□ Yes   □ No   □ Not sure

22. Does your organization have a clearly recognized and understood *driving force* (e.g., products, markets served, technology, natural resources, low cost production, profit/return, distribution/sales, capacity)?

□ Yes   □ No   □ Not sure

23. Identify *one* (1) of the following as your organization's *driving force*:

□ Products

□ Capability for low cost production

□ Markets served

□ Profit/return

□ Distribution/sales process/methodology

□ Technology

□ Natural resources

□ Operational/production capacity

24. Briefly describe or list what, in your opinion, are the most significant elements of the organization's culture (what is important to the organization).

_____

_____

_____

_____

_____

_____

Senior Management Assessment

Organization: _____

Division/unit: _____

Title/position: _____

1. What is the purpose of this organization?

_____

_____

2. What is your current area of responsibility?

_____

3. Does the organization have a vision (strategy) statement?

☐ Yes ☐ No ☐ Not sure

4. Does your division/department have a vision (strategy) statement?

☐ Yes ☐ No ☐ Not sure

5. Can you write a brief statement (without assistance) that summarizes the organization's vision?

☐ Yes ☐ No ☐ Not sure

6. Do your direct reports clearly understand the organization's vision statement?

☐ Yes ☐ No ☐ Not sure

7. Can your direct reports write a brief statement (without assistance) that summarizes the organization's vision?

☐ Yes ☐ No ☐ Not sure

8. Do you refer to the organization's vision statement when making decisions about products, services, customers, users, or markets?

☐ Yes ☐ No ☐ Not sure

9. Do your direct reports refer to the organization's vision statement when making decisions about products, services, customers, users, or markets?

☐ Yes ☐ No ☐ Not sure

10. Did you participate in a process of developing the organization's vision statement?

☐ Yes ☐ No ☐ Not sure

<u>ORGANIZATIONAL VISIONING</u> **2**

11. Have you committed enough time to empowering people in your division/unit to use the vision statement?

☐ Yes   ☐ No   ☐ Not sure

12. What are the three (3) most significant problems facing the organization right now?

_____

_____

_____

13. Does the organization's vision statement help to solve these problems?

☐ Yes   ☐ No   ☐ Not sure

14. Does the organization's vision have internal critics?

☐ Yes   ☐ No   ☐ Not sure

15. Do you know where (departments, job categories, employee types, geographic locations, etc.) the significant critics are located?

☐ Yes   ☐ No   ☐ Not sure

16. In your opinion, is the location/distribution of the key vision critics and their objections directly related to what is bothering them?

☐ Yes   ☐ No   ☐ Not sure

17. Does the organization offer training to employees at all levels, in the use and/or application of the vision to their work?

☐ Yes   ☐ No   ☐ Not sure

18. In your opinion, is all internal and external training related to the use and/or application of the organization's vision?

☐ Yes   ☐ No   ☐ Not sure

19. Does your unit include an evaluation of the use and/or application of the vision in performance appraisals?

☐ Yes   ☐ No   ☐ Not sure

20. Does your organization use a separate process to determine *what* it wants to become (i.e., vision) as opposed to a process that determines *how* to get there (i.e., strategic planning)?

☐ Yes   ☐ No   ☐ Not sure

21. Does your organization have a clearly recognized and understood *driving force* (e.g., products, markets served, technology, natural resources, low cost production, profit/return, distribution/sales, capacity)?

☐ Yes   ☐ No   ☐ Not sure

22. Identify *one* (1) of the following as your organization's *primary business logic*:

☐ Products
☐ Capability for low cost
   production
☐ Markets served
☐ Profit/return

☐ Distribution/sales
   process/methodology
☐ Technology
☐ Natural resources
☐ Operational/production capacity

23. Briefly describe or list what, in your opinion, are the most significant elements of the organization's culture (what is important to the organization).

_____

_____

_____

_____

_____

_____

ORGANIZATIONAL VISIONING **3**

Organization Vision Assessment

Organization: _____

Division/unit: _____

Title/position: _____

1. What is the purpose of the organization?

_____

_____

2. Does the organization have a clearly stated vision statement?

☐ Yes ☐ No ☐ Not sure

3. Is the vision statement formally communicated to all levels of the organization?

☐ Yes ☐ No ☐ Not sure

4. In your opinion, is the vision clearly understood at all levels of the organization?

☐ Yes ☐ No ☐ Not sure

5. Does your particular unit of the organization have a clearly stated vision statement?

☐ Yes ☐ No ☐ Not sure

6. Can you write a brief statement that summarizes the organization's vision?

☐ Yes ☐ No ☐ Not sure

7. Is the organization's vision clearly understood by *your* direct reports?

☐ Yes ☐ No ☐ Not sure

8. Can your direct reports write a brief statement (without assistance) that summarizes the vision statement?

☐ Yes ☐ No ☐ Not sure

9. Do you find the organization's vision statement helpful when making decisions about products, services, customers, users, or markets?

☐ Yes ☐ No ☐ Not sure

10. Do your direct reports refer to the organization's vision statement, and find it helpful when making decisions about products, services, customers, users, or markets?

☐ Yes ☐ No ☐ Not sure

11. Is the organization's vision the result of a process?

☐ Yes ☐ No ☐ Not sure

12. Did you and your direct reports *attempt* to reach consensus regarding the vision and future direction of the organization?

☐ Yes ☐ No ☐ Not sure

13. Did you and your direct reports *reach* consensus regarding the vision and future direction of the organization?

☐ Yes ☐ No ☐ Not sure

14. Does your organization utilize a separate process to determine *what* it wants to become (i.e., visioning) as opposed to a process that determines *how* to get there (i.e., strategic planning)?

☐ Yes ☐ No ☐ Not sure

Vision Needs Assessment

Organization: _____

Division/unit: _____

Title/position: _____

1. What is the purpose of the organization?

_____

_____

2. Does the organization have a vision statement?

☐ Yes ☐ No ☐ Not sure

3. Does the organization have a mission (purpose) statement?

☐ Yes ☐ No ☐ Not sure

4. In your opinion are vision and mission distinctly different ideas?

☐ Yes ☐ No ☐ Not sure

5. If you answered yes to question two, do you believe the vision is clearly understood throughout the organization?

☐ Yes ☐ No ☐ Not sure

6. If you answered no to question two, do you believe the organization needs a vision?

☐ Yes ☐ No ☐ Not sure

7. In your opinion, is there a need to take command of the organization's future?

☐ Yes ☐ No ☐ Not sure

8. In your opinion, is the organization's mission (purpose) clearly understood?

☐ Yes ☐ No ☐ Not sure

9. Is there agreement across the organization on which customers/users have priority?

☐ Yes ☐ No ☐ Not sure

10. Is there agreement on which of the organization's products, services, and technologies are most important?

☐ Yes ☐ No ☐ Not sure

ORGANIZATIONAL VISIONING   **4**

11. Is there agreement on the most significant threats facing the organization?

☐ Yes   ☐ No   ☐ Not sure

12. Is there agreement on the most significant opportunities facing the organization?

☐ Yes   ☐ No   ☐ Not sure

13. In your opinion, are people in the organization unhappy or confused about the current direction of the organization?

☐ Yes   ☐ No   ☐ Not sure

14. In your opinion, are people pessimistic about the future of the organization?

☐ Yes   ☐ No   ☐ Not sure

15. In your opinion, is the organization losing its reputation for:

A. Quality products/services?

☐ Yes   ☐ No   ☐ Not sure

B. Innovation/creativity?

☐ Yes   ☐ No   ☐ Not sure

16. In your opinion, has new or improved competition emerged that better serves your customers/users?

☐ Yes   ☐ No   ☐ Not sure

17. In your opinion, is the organization failing to keep up with:

A. New technology?

☐ Yes   ☐ No   ☐ Not sure

B. Socioeconomic changes?

☐ Yes   ☐ No   ☐ Not sure

C. Political changes?

☐ Yes   ☐ No   ☐ Not sure

D. Environmental conditions and/or changes?

☐ Yes   ☐ No   ☐ Not sure

ORGANIZATIONAL VISIONING   **4**

18. In your opinion, is the organization losing its:

   A. Unique and distinctive reputation?

   ☐ Yes   ☐ No   ☐ Not sure

   B. Sense of pride and commitment among employees?

   ☐ Yes   ☐ No   ☐ Not sure

   C. Desire to accept change?

   ☐ Yes   ☐ No   ☐ Not sure

19. Is the organization faced with significant operational issues or problems that require a new vision?

   ☐ Yes   ☐ No   ☐ Not sure

20. In your opinion, where would the organization be in one to three years if it refuses any changes, and would you like such an outcome?

   Briefly comment: _____

   _____

   _____

   _____

ORGANIZATIONAL VISIONING

Current Organization Profile

Organization: _____

Division/unit: _____

Title/position: _____

1. Please examine the following list of key operational elements. Based on what *you think*, rank them in order of importance to your organization, (1 = most important, 14 = least important).

    ____ Facilities/equipment   ____ Markets (geographic)
    ____ Staff/employees   ____ Income (resources)
    ____ Products   ____ Users/customers
    ____ Services   ____ Advertising/promotion
    ____ Suppliers   ____ Financial reports
    ____ Vendors   ____ Research and development
    ____ Markets (demographic)   ____ Other

2. What are the current key products and/or services your organization provides?

    _____

    _____

    _____

3. Are the current key products and/or services grouped in any way?

    ☐ Yes   ☐ No

    Briefly describe: _____

    _____

    _____

    _____

4. Do current trends and cycles affect the current key products and/or services?

    ☐ Yes   ☐ No

    Briefly describe: _____

    _____

    _____

    _____

ORGANIZATIONAL VISIONING **5**

5. Is there a *principal factor* that determines the products and/or services your organization offers?

☐ Yes ☐ No

Briefly describe: _____

_____

_____

_____

6. Is there a *principal factor* that determines the products and/or services your organization does not offer?

☐ Yes ☐ No

Briefly describe: _____

_____

_____

_____

7. To the best of your ability, identify the users/customers that are attracted to these products/services?

Products/services	Groups
_____	_____
_____	_____
_____	_____
_____	_____
_____	_____

8. Based on available information, what has been the percent of growth in sales for these products/services during the past three years?

Products/services	Percent of growth
_____	_____
_____	_____
_____	_____
_____	_____
_____	_____

9. What is the current percent of market share for these products/services?

Products/services	Percent of market share
_____	_____
_____	_____
_____	_____
_____	_____
_____	_____
_____	_____

10. Is there a _principal factor_ that determines the users or customers the organization seeks?

☐ Yes ☐ No

Briefly describe: _____

_____

_____

_____

11. Is there a _principal factor_ that determines the users or customers the organization does not seek?

☐ Yes ☐ No

Briefly describe: _____

_____

_____

_____

12. What geographic areas does the organization serve?

Products/services	Area
_____	_____
_____	_____
_____	_____
_____	_____
_____	_____
_____	_____

ORGANIZATIONAL VISIONING **5**

13. What demographic markets does the organization serve?

Products/services	Demographic markets
_____	_____
_____	_____
_____	_____
_____	_____
_____	_____
_____	_____

14. Is there a *principal factor* that determines the geographic markets the organization seeks?

☐ Yes   ☐ No

Briefly describe: _____

_____

_____

_____

15. Is there a *principal factor* that determines the geographic markets the organization does not seek?

☐ Yes   ☐ No

Briefly describe: _____

_____

_____

_____

16. Is there a *principal factor* that determines the demographic markets the organization seeks?

☐ Yes   ☐ No

Briefly describe: _____

_____

_____

_____

ORGANIZATIONAL VISIONING   **5**

17. Is there a *principal factor* that determines the demographic markets the organization does not seek?

☐ Yes   ☐ No

Briefly describe: _____

_____

_____

_____

18. Is there a *principal factor* that determines the market segments the organization seeks?

☐ Yes   ☐ No

Briefly describe: _____

_____

_____

_____

19. Is there a *principal factor* that determines the markets segments the organization does not seek?

☐ Yes   ☐ No

Briefly describe: _____

_____

_____

_____

20. Which of the following best describes the organizational structure of the organization?

_____ Pyramid
_____ Hierarchical
_____ Flat
_____ Horizontal

Others, such as:

_____ Inverted pyramid (Pepsi-Cola)
_____ Network
_____ Starburst (Quinn)
_____ Shamrock (Handy)
_____ Pizza (Eastman)

ORGANIZATIONAL VISIONING (5)

21. Based on available information, what is the rate of return for each of the product and/or service divisions in the organization?

Product/service division	Rate of return
_____	_____
_____	_____
_____	_____
_____	_____
_____	_____
_____	_____

22. Identify one (only one) of the following that, in *your judgment*, is the current driving force* of the organization.

☐ User/customer
☐ Product/service
☐ Market
☐ Facility/capacity
☐ Technology
☐ Marketing method
☐ Distribution method
☐ Size/growth
☐ Natural resources
☐ Return/profit

23. In *your opinion*, what is the principal skill, capability, or area of expertise and/or competence that the organization possesses at a level of proficiency higher than anything else it does?

_____

_____

_____

_____

_____

_____

ORGANIZATIONAL VISIONING **5**

24. At this time, do you believe there are critical issues or problems that the organization must face and attempt to change and solve? An example might be "focus of future business development" or "the future mix of products and markets." In any case, you are suggesting a critical issue to be considered during the visioning process.

Critical issue	Change needed
_____	_____
_____	_____
_____	_____
_____	_____
_____	_____
_____	_____
_____	_____
_____	_____
_____	_____
_____	_____

*A driving force is defined as the single most important force, or motive that drives the organization's strategy and gives it its particular identity.

ORGANIZATIONAL VISIONING **6**

Strategic Profile Assessment

Organization: _____

Division/unit: _____

Title/position: _____

1. What is the organization's current strategy?

   Please describe: _____

   _____

   _____

2. In your opinion, is the organization experiencing difficulty implementing the current strategy?

   ☐ Yes   ☐ No   ☐ Not sure

3. The organization's average annual growth in sales/income (real growth) over the next three years will be:

   ☐ Better   ☐ Worse   ☐ No change

4. What major factors will influence growth in your industry during the next three to five years? (Rank choices by degree of influence, 1 being most influential).

   ____ New products   ____ Economic changes

   ____ New services   ____ Demographic changes

   ____ Productivity improvements   ____ New legislation

   (technology/process)   ____ Other (please describe):

   ____ Manufacturing costs   _____

5. How will companies in your industry grow during the next three to five years? (Rank choices by significance, 1 being most significant).

   ____ Application of new technology

   ____ Diversification into new product lines

   ____ Expand services provided to customers

   ____ Geographic expansion

   ____ Acquisition or merger

   ____ Development of new markets

   ____ Increase in export sales

   ____ Manufacturing of products offshore

   ____ Other (please describe):

ORGANIZATIONAL VISIONING

6. Evaluate the importance of the following products and/or services that the organization provides. Select and rank the ten (10) *most important* (1 is most important). Do not duplicate any scores. Add choices as appropriate. In addition, estimate the percentage of the competition that provides the same product or service.

Product or service	Ranking top ten	% of competitors providing
Product design or development		
Custom products	_____	_____
Related supplies	_____	_____
Characteristics (e.g., faster, lighter, etc.)	_____	_____
Training	_____	_____
Other	_____	_____
Product quality		
Quality control	_____	_____
Technical assistance	_____	_____
Replacement parts	_____	_____
Service personnel	_____	_____
Service contracts	_____	_____
Product warranties	_____	_____
Other	_____	_____
Inventory management		
Inventory control	_____	_____
Order handling	_____	_____
Shipping services	_____	_____
On-time delivery	_____	_____
Other	_____	_____
Financial management		
Financial services	_____	_____
Flexible financial terms	_____	_____
Volume discounts	_____	_____
Select customers	_____	_____
Other	_____	_____
Promotional		
Advertising	_____	_____
Promotional events	_____	_____
Other	_____	_____
Customer service		
800 telephone number	_____	_____
Customer service personnel	_____	_____
Training	_____	_____
Other	_____	_____

Products

7. In your opinion, do the current products or services have common characteristics?

☐ Yes   ☐ No

Please list: _____

_____

_____

8. In your opinion, does the organization have any products or services that are exceptionally successful?

☐ Yes   ☐ No

Please list: _____

_____

_____

9. Can the exceptional success of a product or service be attributed to a particular strength or skill?

☐ Yes   ☐ No

Please list: _____

_____

_____

10. In your opinion, does the organization have any products or services that are exceptionally unsuccessful?

☐ Yes   ☐ No

Please list: _____

_____

_____

11. Can the exceptionally poor performance of a product or service be explained?

☐ Yes   ☐ No

Briefly explain: _____

_____

_____

Marketing

12. Do the organization's geographic markets share any common characteristics?

☐ Yes   ☐ No

Please list: _____

_____

_____

13. In your opinion, does the organization have any geographic markets that are exceptionally successful?

☐ Yes   ☐ No

Please list: _____

_____

_____

14. Can the exceptional performance be attributed to a particular strength or skill?

☐ Yes   ☐ No

Briefly explain: _____

_____

_____

15. In your opinion, does the organization have any geographic markets that are exceptionally unsuccessful?

☐ Yes   ☐ No

Please list: _____

_____

_____

16. Can the exceptionally poor performance be explained?

☐ Yes   ☐ No

Briefly explain: _____

_____

_____

ORGANIZATIONAL VISIONING   **6**

17. Do the organization's current customers (customer groups) share any common characteristics?

☐ Yes   ☐ No

Please list: _____

_____

_____

18. In your opinion, does the organization have a customer group that it is exceptionally successful in serving?

☐ Yes   ☐ No

Please list: _____

_____

_____

19. Can this exceptional success be explained?

☐ Yes   ☐ No

Briefly explain: _____

_____

_____

20. In your opinion, does the organization have a customer group that it serves exceptionally unsuccessfully?

☐ Yes   ☐ No

Please list: _____

_____

_____

21. Can this exceptionally poor performance be explained?

☐ Yes   ☐ No

Briefly explain: _____

_____

_____

22. In your opinion, are there trends in the environment that may become threats and/or lost opportunities if the organization's current strategy continues?

☐ Yes   ☐ No

Briefly explain: _____

_____

_____

Organizational Strengths

23. Evaluate the importance of the following success factors for organizations in *your industry*. Select and rank order the ten (10) most important, 1 being most important and 10 being the least important. Do not duplicate any scores. Add choices as appropriate. In addition, rank your organization's performance using the same success factor.

Success factor	Ranking for industry	Your organization's ranking
Product quality	_____	_____
Product availability	_____	_____
Customer service quality	_____	_____
Service availability	_____	_____
Pricing structure	_____	_____
Brand name	_____	_____
Market share	_____	_____
Management information systems	_____	_____
Marketing	_____	_____
Sales	_____	_____
Breadth of product line	_____	_____
Locations	_____	_____
Flexible production capabilities	_____	_____
Sale terms (discounts, etc.)	_____	_____
Productivity	_____	_____
Other:	_____	_____
	_____	_____
	_____	_____
	_____	_____
	_____	_____

ORGANIZATIONAL VISIONING **6**

24. Please list the organization's values (culture), which in your judgment, significantly influence the daily action/behavior of employees.

_____

_____

_____

_____

_____

25. In your opinion, does the organization have any _unique_ strengths?

☐ Yes   ☐ No

Please list: _____

_____

_____

26. In your opinion, does the organization possess any of these strengths to a greater extent than the competitors?

☐ Yes   ☐ No

Please list: _____

_____

_____

27. In your opinion, are there any current organizational _traits or elements_ that may become future strengths?

☐ Yes   ☐ No

Please list: _____

_____

_____

28. In your opinion, does the organization's attempt to implement the current strategy reveal significant under-utilized strengths and/or weaknesses?

☐ Yes   ☐ No   ☐ Not sure

Briefly explain: _____

_____

_____

ORGANIZATIONAL VISIONING   **6**

Organizational Weaknesses

29. In your opinion, does the organization have any *unique* weaknesses?

☐ Yes   ☐ No

Please list: _____

_____

_____

30. Does the organization possess any of these weaknesses to a greater extent than the competitors?

☐ Yes   ☐ No

Please list: _____

_____

_____

31. In your opinion, are there any current organizational *traits* that may become future weaknesses?

☐ Yes   ☐ No

Please list: _____

_____

_____

32. In your opinion, does the organization's current strategy require greater competence and/or resources than it possesses?

☐ Yes   ☐ No   ☐ Not sure

Briefly explain: _____

_____

_____

ORGANIZATIONAL VISIONING **6**

33. Rank the ten (10) most important factors that have a major impact on the organization, but are beyond its control. Base your ranking on 1 being the most important and 10 being the least important.

Factors	Ranking of top ten
Technology	
Computer applications	_____
Information systems	_____
Product innovation	_____
Warehouse technology	_____
Production automation	_____
Other	_____
Economics	
Disposable income	_____
Construction starts	_____
Currency rates	_____
Interest rates	_____
Inflation	_____
Commodity prices	_____
Unemployment	_____
Health care	_____
Other	_____
Market/demographics	
Competitor strategies	_____
Cyclical nature of industry	_____
New competition	_____
Foreign competition	_____
Population trends	_____
Supplier strategies	_____
Other	_____
Financial management	
Local taxes	_____
State taxes	_____
Federal taxes	_____
Product licensing	_____
Import/export laws	_____
Labor laws and regulations	_____
Other	_____

ORGANIZATIONAL VISIONING **7**

Competitor Assessment

Company: _____

Division/unit: _____

Title/position: _____

1. In your opinion, who are the organization's most significant competitors?

   A. _____   E. _____

   B. _____   F. _____

   C. _____   G. _____

   D. _____   H. _____

2. What are the key strategies these competitors use?

Organization	**Strategy**
A. _____	_____
B. _____	_____
C. _____	_____
D. _____	_____
E. _____	_____
F. _____	_____
G. _____	_____
H. _____	_____

3. How important are the strategies in question two to current competitors? Will current competitors continue to invest in these strategies?

Organization's strategy	**Importance**	**Continued investment**
A. _____	_____	_____
B. _____	_____	_____
C. _____	_____	_____
D. _____	_____	_____
E. _____	_____	_____
F. _____	_____	_____
G. _____	_____	_____
H. _____	_____	_____

4. What changes in the competitor's strategies are likely in the near future?

Organization's changes in strategy

A. _____

B. _____

C. _____

D. _____

E. _____

F. _____

G. _____

H. _____

5. What weaknesses do the competitors have? What strengths?

Organization's weakness	Strength
A. _____	_____
B. _____	_____
C. _____	_____
D. _____	_____
E. _____	_____
F. _____	_____
G. _____	_____
H. _____	_____

6. In your opinion, what are the implications of the competitor's strategies to the organization?

Organization's strategy	Implication
A. _____	_____
B. _____	_____
C. _____	_____
D. _____	_____
E. _____	_____
F. _____	_____
G. _____	_____
H. _____	_____

7. Using the scale provided below, rank the organization against each competitor on the basis of the criteria listed.

1 Superior to   **2** Better than   **3** Equal to   **4** Worse than   **5** Inferior to

Category	A	B	C	D	E	F	G	H
Finance								
Current ratio	___	___	___	___	___	___	___	___
Debt/equity ratio	___	___	___	___	___	___	___	___
Inventory turnover	___	___	___	___	___	___	___	___
Margin	___	___	___	___	___	___	___	___
Sales per employee	___	___	___	___	___	___	___	___
Production								
Product life cycle	___	___	___	___	___	___	___	___
Capacity	___	___	___	___	___	___	___	___
Productivity	___	___	___	___	___	___	___	___
Location	___	___	___	___	___	___	___	___
Obsolescence	___	___	___	___	___	___	___	___
Quality control	___	___	___	___	___	___	___	___
Technology								
Production	___	___	___	___	___	___	___	___
R & D budget	___	___	___	___	___	___	___	___
R & D capabilities	___	___	___	___	___	___	___	___
Information systems	___	___	___	___	___	___	___	___
Patent position	___	___	___	___	___	___	___	___
Organization								
Staff-to-line ratio	___	___	___	___	___	___	___	___
Quality of staff	___	___	___	___	___	___	___	___
Quality of management	___	___	___	___	___	___	___	___
Quality of sales force	___	___	___	___	___	___	___	___
Communication	___	___	___	___	___	___	___	___
Marketing								
Price	___	___	___	___	___	___	___	___
Market share	___	___	___	___	___	___	___	___
Product reputation	___	___	___	___	___	___	___	___
Product line	___	___	___	___	___	___	___	___
Advertising efficiency	___	___	___	___	___	___	___	___
Customer complaints	___	___	___	___	___	___	___	___
Dist. channel efficiency	___	___	___	___	___	___	___	___
Personnel								
Mgmt. succession	___	___	___	___	___	___	___	___
Turnover	___	___	___	___	___	___	___	___

ORGANIZATIONAL VISIONING **8**

Competitor Assessment: Key Questions

1. Who is the competition now?

_____

_____

2. Who will it be in one year, three years, five years?

_____

_____

3. What are the key competitor's visions, strategies, objectives, and goals?

_____

_____

4. How important are specific markets to competitors, and are they committed enough to continue investing in them?

_____

_____

5. What unique strengths do competitors have?

_____

_____

6. Do competitors have any weaknesses that make them vulnerable?

_____

_____

7. What changes are likely in these competitor's future strategies?

_____

_____

8. What are the implications of the competitor's strategies on the industry, market, and your organization?

_____

_____

ORGANIZATIONAL VISIONING

Competitor Information Sources

1. What is your competition saying about themselves?

Public

- Advertising
- Promotional materials
- Speeches
- Books
- Articles
- Personnel changes
- Employment ads
- Executive searches
- Press releases

Trade/Professional

- Manuals
- Licenses
- Patents
- Technical papers
- Courses
- Seminars

Investors

- Annual meetings
- Annual reports
- Prospectuses
- Stock/bond issues

Government

- Securities and exchange reports
- FIC
- Legislation
- Court testimony
- Litigation
- Lawsuit records
- Antitrust actions

ORGANIZATIONAL VISIONING

2. What are others saying about your competition?

Public

- Case studies
- Books
- Articles
- Newspapers
- Consultants
- Consumer groups
- Unions
- Recruitment/search firms
- Environmental groups

Trade/Professional

- Trade publications
- Industry studies
- Customers
- Users
- Suppliers
- Vendors
- Subcontractors
- Professional organizations

Investors

- Securities analysts
- Security reports
- Credit reports
- Industry data

Government

- Litigation
- Lawsuit records
- State agencies
- Federal agencies
- International agencies
- Antitrust actions
- Government programs

PART IV

VISUAL PRESENTATION

For Presentation and Discussion

THIS PART OF THE BOOK provides examples of visual materials that may help the facilitator and the organization with the presentation of the recommended sessions listed in the Methodology for Vision Development. These visuals provide a summary of the information from Part I.

VISUAL MATERIALS TITLE OUTLINE

Building a Shared Vision: A Leaders Guide to Aligning the Organization
Characteristics of Success
Terminology
Organizational Visioning Topics
    Building a Shared Vision
    What Is Shared Vision?
        Hickman and Silva Quote
    Why Do It?
        Disney Quote
        Leacock Quote
        The Need for Vision

Phase IV: Recognizing the Obstacles
    Do the Leaders Believe in It?
    Is It Clearly Understood?
    Have You Compared the *Old* and *New*?
    How Will the New Vision Affect the Organization?
    How Will the New Vision Affect the Competition?
    Exercises for Recognizing the Obstacles (2)
Phase V: Implementation—Vision in Action
    Action and Commitment
    Internal Tools (3)
    Making It Happen (3)
Phase VI: Continous Vision Improvement
Organizational Visioning Graphic

Building a Shared Vision

A Leader's Guide to Aligning the Organization

Characteristics of success

The three most significant characteristics of successful leaders and their organizations include:

☐ Vision
☐ Willingness to learn
☐ Commitment to continuous improvement

2

Terminology

☐ Constituencies/stakeholders
☐ Current organization audit
☐ Driving force
☐ Hard/soft data
☐ Mission
☐ Organization variables assessment

☐ Purpose
☐ Strategic planning
☐ Values/culture
☐ Vision

3

Organizational visioning topics

☐ Building a shared vision
☐ What is shared vision?
☐ Why do it?
☐ Where do you begin?
☐ What roles do people play?
☐ Getting where you want to go

4

Building a shared vision

☐ The driving force
☐ New realities
☐ Looking to the future
☐ What do we want to create?

5

What is shared vision?

☐ Examples
☐ Definition and framework
☐ Organizational strengths
☐ What the organization should look
   like, feel like, be like, achieve

6

What is shared vision?

"*Vision is a key component of leadership;
it is that mental journey from the known to
the unknown, creating the future from the
montage of current facts, hopes, dreams,
risks, and opportunities that effective
leaders embrace in all walks of life.*"

—Hickman and Silva, *Creating Excellence*

7

*W*HY DO IT?

The need for vision

☐ Does the organization have a clear vision statement?

☐ Do key people disagree over purpose?

☐ Does the organization appear to have lost its
- Unique/distinctive reputation?
- Pride and commitment?
- Interest in risk and change?

☐ Is the organization keeping up with external changes?

11

*W*HY DO IT?

Forces put in motion by vision

☐ Work takes on greater meaning

☐ Increased commitment, motivation and energy

☐ Connects people and jobs

☐ Awareness of organization's competencies, what it stands for, where it's headed

☐ Activities/objectives/goals reflect what it wants to create

☐ Risk taking, creativity, innovation

☐ A tool for evaluation

12

Where do you begin?

The goal is a vision that will:

☐ Identify opportunities

☐ Exploit opportunities

☐ Be ambitious and look to future

☐ Reflect uniqueness

☐ Improve job satisfaction

☐ Set high standards

☐ Generate commitment, excitement, pride

☐ Clarify new direction

13

Where do you begin? (cont.)

☐ Learn
☐ Think about tomorrow
☐ Who must buy in?
☐ What is the target?
☐ Focus on success
☐ Resources
☐ Top-down?

14

WHERE DO YOU BEGIN?

Learn

☐ Business/industry   ☐ Values/culture
☐ Past/current vision   ☐ Strengths/weakness
☐ Mission   ☐ Uniqueness
☐ Structure   ☐ What's needed to succeed

15

WHERE DO YOU BEGIN?

Think about tomorrow

☐ Future business developments
☐ Changes in markets/products
☐ Changes in stakeholders/constituencies
☐ External environment—economic, social, technical, political

16

*W*HERE DO YOU BEGIN?

Who must buy in?

- ☐ Board members
- ☐ Investors
- ☐ Staff/employees
- ☐ Customers
- ☐ Suppliers
- ☐ Community

17

*W*HERE DO YOU BEGIN?

What is the target?

- ☐ What should the organization/unit be doing?
- ☐ What must be achieved?
- ☐ What issues must be addressed?

18

*W*HERE DO YOU BEGIN?

Focus on success

- ☐ Concentrate less on incremental processes—more on grand results
- ☐ An effort that only this organization has capability to achieve

19

---

*W*HERE DO YOU BEGIN?

Resources
- ☐ Prepare to invest resources
- ☐ Success depends on key people, money, facilities, employees, materials, etc.

Top-down?
- ☐ Be ready to abandon belief in vision as a top-down statement; or
- ☐ That planning staff and process are the vision source

20

What roles do people play?

- ☐ Organization has the opportunity for:
  - • Collective action/synergy
  - • Multilevel participation in development and implementation of vision
- ☐ Shared vision is the expression of what individuals care about with opportunities to ultimately create a new tomorrow

---

*W*HAT ROLES DO PEOPLE PLAY?

"There are two things which the top management must keep in mind...
The first task... is to create a vision that gives meaning to the employees' jobs.
The second task is to constantly convey a sense of crisis to their employees."

—President Kaku, Canon

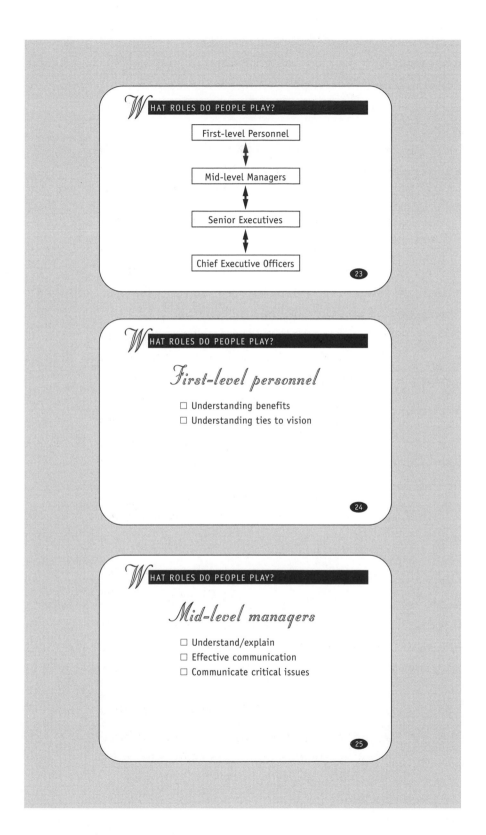

WHAT ROLES DO PEOPLE PLAY?

Senior executives

- ☐ Development/articulation
- ☐ Demonstrate and communicate commitment
- ☐ Decisions reflect vision
- ☐ Equal time

26

WHAT ROLES DO PEOPLE PLAY?

Chief executive officers

- ☐ Leadership
- ☐ Open to diversity
- ☐ Change agent
- ☐ Negotiator/cheerleader
- ☐ Mentor/model
- ☐ Consistent decisions
- ☐ Open mind
- ☐ Plan adjustments
- ☐ Performance evaluation/ reward system

27

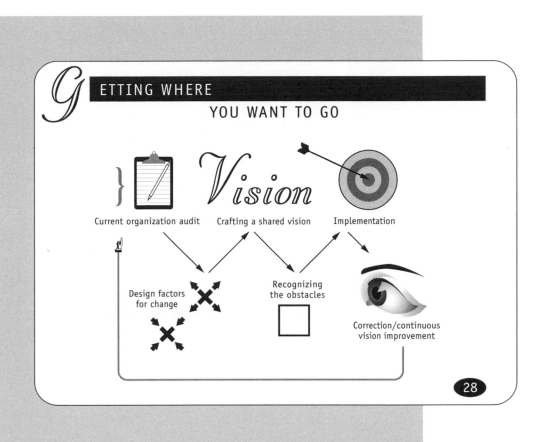

---

*G*ETTING WHERE YOU WANT TO GO

Limitations of "hard" data

☐ Limited in scope, richness; fails to include noneconomic/nonquantitative factors
☐ Too aggregated for effective use in strategy/vision development
☐ Much of it comes too late for use in strategy/vision development
☐ Surprising amount is unreliable

29

---

*G*ETTING WHERE YOU WANT TO GO

Problems with "soft" data

☐ Speculative
☐ Relies on human memory
☐ Subject to psychological distortions

30

---

*G*ETTING WHERE YOU WANT TO GO

Hard vs. soft data

☐ Ideally, vision draws on both sources of information
☐ Hard data may inform
☐ Soft data generate wisdom

31

PHASE I:

Current organization audit

☐ Does the organization have a vision statement?
☐ Can executives/managers write a brief statement of the vision?
☐ Does the organization have a mission/purpose statement?
☐ Identify strengths, weaknesses, special skills
☐ Identify organization's unique characteristic or competence

32

PHASE I:

Current organization audit (cont.)

☐ Describe scope of current products, services, markets, customers
☐ What current products, services, markets, and customers will be dropped in the future?
☐ Are there plans for new products, services, markets, and customers?
☐ What distinguishes the organization's products and services?

33

PHASE I:

Current organization audit (cont.)

☐ Are current structures, processes, policies, and information systems adequate?
☐ Do key people *know* the direction and *agree*?
☐ What is the current driving force?

34

PHASE II:

Preparing for change

☐ What are the key issues?

☐ Who must be satisfied?

☐ How will everyone know when they get there?

☐ Will there be limitations?

☐ Control of competitive arena

☐ Become futurists

---

*P*HASE II: PREPARING FOR CHANGE

What are the key issues?

☐ What will be the *direction* of future business development?

☐ What future range of products, services, and markets will be *considered*?

☐ How will current and future products, services, and markets *differ*?

☐ Will future products, services, and markets be prioritized so resources will be focused on the *vision*?

---

*P*HASE II: PREPARING FOR CHANGE

What are the key issues? (*cont.*)

☐ Are key capabilities and resources needed for shared vision to succeed?

☐ Effect of shared vision on expected growth and return

*P*HASE II: PREPARING FOR CHANGE

Who must the organization satisfy?

☐ Internal/external constituencies that
  have stake in organization's future
☐ List and rank critical constituencies
☐ What are the primary interests and
  expectations of each one?

38

*P*HASE II: PREPARING FOR CHANGE

*How will everyone know
when they get there?*

☐ Shared vision commits everyone to
  evaluation criteria they created
☐ Carefully thought-out evaluation process
  and procedure
☐ Keep everyone accurately informed about
  the soundness of the information and
  assumptions the vision was based on

39

*P*HASE II: PREPARING FOR CHANGE

*How will everyone know
when they get there? (cont.)*

☐ In the design of evaluation process, keep
  the following in mind:
  • Impact of vision and accountability for
    all decisions and actions
  • What key points will determine if
    vision is on/off target?
  • Is organization working with customers/
    users/suppliers as vision states?

40

*P*HASE II: PREPARING FOR CHANGE

How will everyone know when they get there? (cont.)

☐ How will people know if they are working with each other as the vision states?

☐ Senior executives must know how they and direct reports are doing

☐ Everyone consistently informed about how well *they* and organization are doing

☐ Routinely schedule vision review and evaluation sessions

41

*P*HASE II: PREPARING FOR CHANGE

Will there be limitations?

☐ What will/will not be included?

☐ Time frames

☐ Geographical limits

☐ Future social, political, economic realities

☐ Financial limits

42

*P*HASE II: PREPARING FOR CHANGE

How do you control the competitive arena?

☐ How comprehensive is the competition's strategy (product-centered, process-centered, structurally oriented)?

☐ Identify all real or potential changes in competition

☐ Develop scenarios that anticipate competition's response and strategy due to new vision

☐ How do competitors view the future?

43

HASE II: PREPARING FOR CHANGE

How do you control the competitive arena? (cont.)

- ☐ How are competitors positioning themselves to respond to potential futures (extension, reinvention, etc.)?
- ☐ What are the sources of competition's ideas for future direction?
- ☐ How can this information be used to develop/refine the vision?

 44

 HASÉ II: PREPARING FOR CHANGE

How do you control the competitive arena? (cont.)

- ☐ Is there a need to be competitive?
- ☐ Use this information to develop a plan to manage competition's strategy

45

HASE II: PREPARING FOR CHANGE

How do you become a futurist?

- ☐ If you could create it, what future would you create?
- ☐ What future developments will influence the organization and vision statement?
- ☐ List expectations, based on vision time frame, for each development
- ☐ Prioritize expectations that will impact vision statement

 46

PHASE II: PREPARING FOR CHANGE

How do you become a futurist? (cont.)

- ☐ Be curious
- ☐ Examine outside fields, business, and industries
- ☐ A lot of ideas—too much is not enough
- ☐ Don't be afraid to be led astray
- ☐ Break up your routine
- ☐ Pay attention to a wide variety of information
- ☐ Do not ignore the obvious
- ☐ Use a magnifying glass

47

PHASE II: PREPARING FOR CHANGE

How do you become a futurist? (cont.)

- ☐ Stand back—look at the big picture
- ☐ Remember where you have been
- ☐ Write down the vision when you discover it

48

PHASE III:
Crafting a shared vision

- ☐ Knowledge is important
- ☐ Role of driving force/logic
- ☐ Prioritize vision options
- ☐ Agree on the best
- ☐ Prepare statement that focuses on the future and inspires enthusiasm and commitment

49

HASE III: CRAFTING A SHARED VISION

Knowledge is important

- ☐ Review all information/materials that have been compiled
- ☐ Knowledge is source for insight for crafting shared vision
- ☐ Be flexible and receptive to ideas, intuition, insights, regardless of source

50

HASE III: CRAFTING A SHARED VISION

Driving force/logic

- ☐ Logic/element/motive that gives the organization special identity
- ☐ Can be key factor affecting future direction and vision

51

HASE III: CRAFTING A SHARED VISION

Driving force/logic (cont.)

- ☐ Only one (1) of the following serves as primary source of organization's force/logic

- Products/service offered
- Users/customers
- Markets served
- Low-cost production, capability, capacity
- Marketing/sales methods
- Technology
- Method of distribution
- Return/profit
- Size/growth
- Natural resources

52

HASE III: CRAFTING A SHARED VISION

Ranking the options

☐ Develop list of prioritized shared visions
☐ Test each potential vision against vision success factors
☐ Is there consistency with strengths, driving forces, culture, and values?
☐ Is change a higher priority?

53

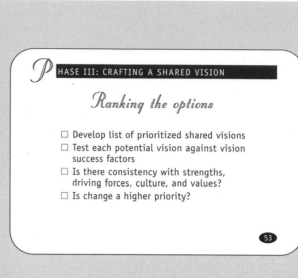**HASE III: CRAFTING A SHARED VISION**

Choosing the best

☐ Select and test again the highest ranking vision from priority list
☐ Put it into a statement that focuses on:
  • Exciting future
  • Value creating
  • High ideals, standards, and uniqueness of organization
  • Providing decision-making criteria that are clear
  • Inspiring enthusiasm and commitment

54

HASE III: CRAFTING A SHARED VISION

Crafting the vision

☐ Put vision in different contexts (historical, futuristic, political, economic, etc.)
☐ Make list of what-if questions; go as far out as you can
☐ Look at vision backwards, upside down, etc.
☐ How much can you combine with the vision?
☐ Create a metaphor for the vision

55

*P*HASE III: CRAFTING A SHARED VISION

Crafting the vision (cont.)

☐ Eliminate rules, the obsolete, the unnecessary
☐ Poke fun at the vision; roast it and create jokes using it
☐ Let vision incubate

56

PHASE IV:
Recognizing the obstacles

Take the time to ask:

☐ Is this the best vision?
☐ What are the chances for success?
☐ If it fails, what can we salvage?
☐ Should we try?

57

*P*HASE IV: RECOGNIZING THE OBSTACLES

Do the leaders believe in it?

☐ Is it right for the internal and external environments?
☐ Is it right for everyone who will interact with it?
☐ Will it lead to improved performances?

58

PHASE IV: RECOGNIZING THE OBSTACLES

Is it clearly understood?

☐ Use small-group sounding board
☐ Informal discussions and meetings
☐ Printed materials
☐ Bulletin boards
☐ Formal general meetings

59

PHASE IV: RECOGNIZING THE OBSTACLES

*Have you compared the
old and new?*

☐ Are they far apart?
☐ What changes will be required?
☐ Will new resources, suppliers, and skills be needed?
☐ Is time frame realistic?
☐ Does new vision need modification?

60

PHASE IV: RECOGNIZING THE OBSTACLES

*How will the new vision
affect the organization?*

☐ Maximize its strength—minimize its weakness
☐ Does it challenge current culture?
☐ Does it respond to current and future opportunities and threats?

61

PHASE IV: RECOGNIZING THE OBSTACLES

How will the new vision affect the competition?

- ☐ Does it challenge strength and exploit weakness of competition?
- ☐ How will competition react?
- ☐ What is competition's strategy and what drives it?
- ☐ Does it counteract competition's expertise and competence?

62

PHASE IV: RECOGNIZING THE OBSTACLES

Exercises for recognizing the obstacles

- ☐ What is the vision attempting to do?
- ☐ Does the vision have drawbacks?
- ☐ What are the chances for success?
- ☐ What can be saved if it fails?
- ☐ Is this the right time for the vision?
- ☐ When is decision needed?

63

PHASE IV: RECOGNIZING THE OBSTACLES

Exercises for recognizing the obstacles (cont.)

- ☐ What assumptions is it based on?
- ☐ Are the assumptions still sound?
- ☐ Is everyone aware of all the assumptions?
- ☐ Are previous successes preventing seeing any problems in the vision?
- ☐ What is the decision?

64

PHASE V:

Implementation—Vision in action

Action and commitment

☐ Action gives it life
☐ Commitment needed if people are to buy in and understand what it means personally
☐ CEO and senior management must demonstrate personal commitment
☐ CEO and senior management apply vision to all actions and decisions
☐ Look for opportunities to communicate vision 65

---

*P*HASE V: IMPLEMENTATION—VISION IN ACTION

Action and commitment (cont.)

☐ Management at all levels must communicate significance of vision
☐ Vision doomed if management fails to reinforce it
- Enthusiasm
- Coaching
- Role models

66

---

*P*HASE V: IMPLEMENTATION—VISION IN ACTION

Internal tools

☐ Performance appraisal system
☐ Personnel policies
☐ Organization culture

67

PHASE V: IMPLEMENTATION—VISION IN ACTION

Internal tools (cont.)

- ☐ Role of performance appraisal systems
  - People on notice to use vision
  - There will be evaluation-feedback-reward
- ☐ Role of personnel policies
  - Complementary mechanisms
  - Recruitment
  - Orientation
  - Training
  - Compensation guidelines

68

PHASE V: IMPLEMENTATION—VISION IN ACTION

Internal tools (cont.)

- ☐ Role of organization culture
  - Identifies what is "right"
  - Shaped/reshaped to support vision
  - Activities include rewards, team building, orientation, training
- ☐ Combination of commitment, communication, appraisal systems, personnel policies, and culture makes an important difference

69

PHASE V: IMPLEMENTATION—VISION IN ACTION

Making it happen

- ☐ What are the qualities that will enable you to implement the vision?
- ☐ What is the strategy?
- ☐ What is the motivation?
- ☐ What can be sacrificed?
- ☐ What are the consequences of failure?

70

*P*HASE V: IMPLEMENTATION—VISION IN ACTION

Making it happen (cont.)

☐ What could prevent getting started?
☐ Name five people who will help implement the vision
☐ What skills are needed to implement?
☐ What criticism of the vision can be expected?

71

*P*HASE V: IMPLEMENTATION—VISION IN ACTION

Making it happen (cont.)

☐ What obstacles could get in the way?
☐ Can needless battles be avoided?
☐ What was accomplished?
☐ What has been learned?

72

PHASE VI:

Continuous vision improvement

☐ Evaluation and refinement of the vision
☐ Evaluation based on performance of vision for specified time
☐ Review steps involved in crafting the vision
☐ Review new critical issues
☐ Determine need for revision
☐ Revise/refine vision statement

73

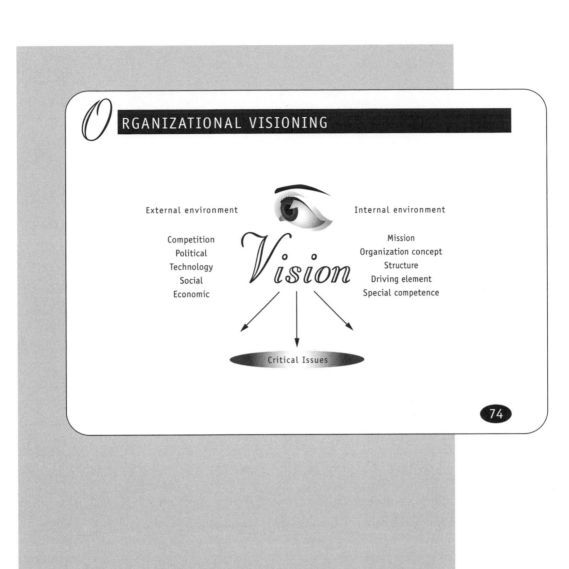

PART V

VISIONING FOR THE INDIVIDUAL, TEAM, OR UNIT

CHAPTER 1

Where Do You Begin?

WHERE DO YOU BEGIN to put into words the shared vision that describes the desired future that you and your work team or unit are willing to craft, get approval for, and implement? It must be a direction that you and your coworkers believe will be good for the team or unit as well as the parent organization. It is also likely that this activity will take place in an organization that has no vision statement yet. Large and complex organizations often find it difficult to develop, let alone articulate, a vision of the future. Nevertheless, even when executives and top management create a vision, it is essential that individual employees, within the framework of the organization's mission and purpose, create their own shared vision of the future.

For many, shared vision begins as something personal, perhaps a dream, a stroke of genius, or simply a "gut feeling." For others it is born of either a combination of intuition and unique insight based on instinct, knowledge, experience, judgment, and imagination, or a continuous and often chaotic process. These values, images, impressions, sensations, or dreams for the future and what people hope to contribute become real only through a more concrete expression.

"Every now and then, a man's mind is stretched by a new idea or sensation, and never shrinks back to its former dimensions."

—Oliver Wendell Holmes, Sr.

THE QUEST

You or the unit must undertake a quest to articulate and implement a powerful and easily understood shared vision that will:

- Identify opportunities others don't see.

- Exploit opportunities that others cannot.

- Be future-oriented and ambitious.

- Reflect your own and your unit's uniqueness accurately.

- Improve job satisfaction.

- Set high standards for productivity and quality.

- Generate personal or unit enthusiasm, commitment, pride, and loyalty.

- Clarify the new direction by defining what individuals and the unit need to make happen.

AN EFFECTIVE START

The process does not begin in a vacuum.

An effective start toward building a clear and focused shared vision requires careful thought and action. Moreover, despite the absence of precise formulas for its creation, the process is much less mystical than we might assume and does not begin in a vacuum. The following steps demystify the process and clarify how to begin.

1. Learn. Learn all you can about your job or position, unit, and organization, and what you and your coworkers need to be successful. An excellent starting point is to ask and answer the question, "What is the purpose of this organization and unit?"

2. Think about tomorrow. Start thinking about tomorrow and the impact of future technological developments.

3. Who must buy in? Identify all of the individuals or groups that you want to have a stake—today and tomorrow—in the development and implementation of the work group's or unit's shared vision. They should include your manager/supervisor, coworkers, and customers. Your ability to attract and enlist these groups depends on what you know and learn about their special interests, goals, and needs.

4. What is the target? Identify the objective of the shared vision. Give careful consideration to:

- What you and the unit should be doing.

- What you and the unit must achieve.

- What critical individual and/or unit issues the vision must address

It is critical to keep in mind the significance of specifically identifying the unit's specific goal and objective.

5. Focus on success. Focus on the essence of success. One of the essential requirements facing individuals in the 1990s is to concentrate as much on grand results as incremental processes. You and every member of your unit must feel part of something that no other group has the capability to achieve.

6. Commitment. Take ownership of your work by crafting and committing to a shared vision that is meaningful to you, your unit, and the organization, and that will achieve something organizationally significant.

7. Top-down? Abandon the belief that shared visions are top-down statements. Vision is necessary at all levels of an organization. Wherever people have control of resources, accept responsibility for certain activities, and commit to making a difference, they should be encouraged to develop and implement a sense of direction personally and within the work unit that is consistent with the organization's vision.

CHAPTER 2

Getting Where You Want to Go

IT IS A SIGNIFICANT OVERSTATEMENT to say that a successful shared vision is always the result of orderly processes. Nevertheless, there are steps that can put into order the key elements that you and your coworkers will find useful in creating your new tomorrow. In the following discussion of these steps, however, keep two factors in mind:

- First, because building a shared vision is such a creative and introspective experience, some people will be extremely uncomfortable with inherent complexities and ambiguities.

- Second, it is essential to remember that shared vision is a qualitative assessment of your function and unit and its present and future environment.

This means much of the data is soft in contrast to the hard data that most planning and analysis processes generate today. While hard data certainly informs, soft data provides the insights and wisdom that become the foundation of an effective shared vision. But, in order to acquire such knowledge and apply it effectively to building your unit's shared vision, you must ask the right questions.

The following phases help you and your coworkers expose, assemble, and collect the impressions, opinions, and creative thinking you need to move the unit from where it currently is to where you want it to go.

PHASE I: CURRENT JOB AUDIT

Building a shared vision starts with a clear understanding of your current job description and responsibilities, as well as the composition, operation, and direction of your unit and the fundamentals of the business the organization is in. To do this, examine the jobs and how they are performed; your users/customers; and the business, financial, and market implications of what you do, and your future if nothing changes. What is the purpose of this work group? The answer to that question marks a critical starting point.

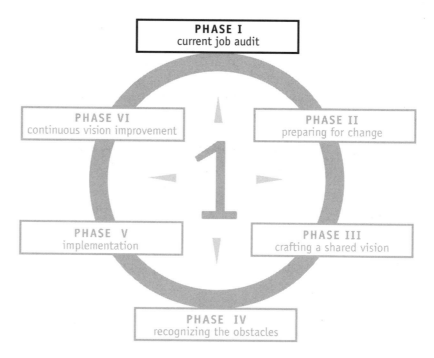

Examples of more questions you need to ask and answer include:

- Do you, or does your unit have a vision?

- Could you write a brief statement of your own, or your work group's vision?

- Does your unit/team have a mission or purpose statement?

- Do you or does your work group have a unique or particular competence?

- What strengths, weaknesses, and areas of special skill do you and your coworkers bring to your jobs, unit, and organization?

- What is the scope of your own and your unit's responsibilities (current products, services, markets, and customers)?

- Using the above categories and lists, can you identify those you believe will be expanded or dropped in the future?

- What distinguishes the unit and the products and/or services it provides?

In addition to a picture of your job in its present state, the answers to these and similar questions provide a focus for responding to all of the threats and opportunities in the internal environment. At this point, you have a framework for your own and the unit's shared vision.

PHASE II: PREPARING FOR CHANGE

Having generated baseline information and determined your own and the unit's need and readiness for shared vision, the next step is to design it.

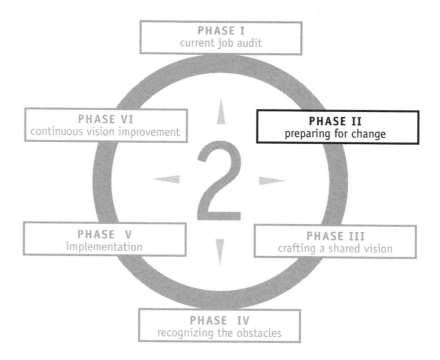

Providing yourself with a vision design that is clear and focused requires thoughtful consideration of the following questions:

What Are the Key Issues?

Everyone has basic issues and concerns that require clarification and total understanding to focus their vision. For example:

- What is the direction of your future job and career development?

- What future range of responsibilities, technical and analytical skills, and new or expanded services will you consider?

- How will the current and future ranges of your job responsibilities and technical and analytical skills differ?

- What key capabilities and resources will you need for your shared vision to succeed?

- How will your shared vision affect your anticipated professional growth?

Who Must You Satisfy?

Every organizational unit has internal and external constituencies made up of individuals, groups, or institutions that have a significant stake in the results of its work. Since each constituency has a particular involvement with you or with the unit, it is likely that their interests, priorities, and expectations will differ. At the same time, constituencies can provide critical insights into the unit's future development and direction. More importantly, they have the power to exert varying degrees of influence on your shared vision. Any one of them could present you with an opportunity or a challenge. Therefore, in order to understand their roles it is important to know as much as possible about each of them. Start by making a list and ranking your critical constituencies. Finally, make an effort to understand each one's primary interests and expectations about your unit's current state and future.

How Will You Know When You Get There?

From the start of the process it is important to remember that your shared vision will be battered and tested externally and internally. The complexities and uncertainties of a tumultuous social, political, and economic future are the primary drivers of external challenges. Meanwhile, internally, you will find yourself accountable for making decisions and taking actions that must be consistent with your shared vision. What you create will become the critical benchmark for measuring your own performance and evaluation. While that may seem easy to do, people in organizations have experienced surprising difficulty working and being evaluated on the basis of rules that they themselves created and accepted. But, that is precisely what must be done. The implementation of the shared vision commits you and your coworkers to a performance evaluation based on self-generated criteria.

> The implementation of your shared vision commits you to a performance evaluation based on criteria you created for yourself.

Feedback is essential.

Obviously, implementing and sustaining your shared vision in the face of these external and internal realities requires, among other things, involvement in a carefully thought-out evaluation process and procedure. Minimally, it should provide you and your co-workers with two significant sources of information. First, whatever the process and procedure, the system must keep everyone accurately informed regarding the soundness of the information and underlying assumptions on which the shared vision was based. This is especially important because the future never happens exactly as forecasted.

When designing an evaluation system, it is important that you keep the following in mind:

- A key to the successful creation and implementation of your own and the unit's shared vision is the extent of its impact on internal accountability for all decisions and actions.

- From a list of assumptions and categories, you should identify and prioritize targets that determine if your shared vision is moving in the right direction.

- You should have ways of knowing if the vision is working with customers/users and suppliers.

- You should have valid and useful data that tell you how you are doing.

- Vision review and evaluation sessions should be routinely scheduled with your supervisor/manager.

Will There Be Limitations?

What will or will not

be included

For your shared vision to clearly express a direction, it should state what will or will not be included. Depending on your job description and responsibilities, time frames, technical restraints, financial realities, as well as the organization's future, cultural and political environment should be considered carefully in every stage of vision creation.

For example, when the introduction of information technology changes the workplace, you and your coworkers must take the initiative, develop your shared vision, and become empowered to act regardless of management's direction. How far into the future your shared vision focuses is influenced by a time limit to become financially literate; acquiring needed group interaction and buy-in; and mastering and implementing the new mathematical, technical, and analytical skills.

If real change is the goal, you and your coworkers must first establish a framework for your shared vision by determining its purpose, benefits, resources needed, and time frame.

How Do You Influence the Internal Competitive Arena?

Organizations are highly competitive environments. That is especially true when resource allocation and budget decisions are determined. One of the marks of an effective shared vision is the extent to which it reflects recognition of how important it is to influence, if not control, the organization's internal competitive arena. But, this can be a difficult task. Keep in mind that organizational restructuring is often a key outcome of implementing change processes which as a result, change internal competition for resources, making it more intense and complex.

Organizations are competitive environments.

The solution lies in responding to the internal competition for resources with a proactive, rather than reactive, shared vision. Here are some suggestions on how to do this:

Be proactive.

- Identify as many real or potential changes as possible in the resource and budget needs of internal competitors.

- Develop a scenario for each internal competitor that anticipates their response and strategy in terms of resources to your unit's shared vision.

- Using this knowledge of the internal competition's strategy, develop your shared vision and follow up with a strategy to manage it.

How Do You Become a Futurist?

People use an assortment of tools that lead them to think they can see into the future: market research, scenario planning, forecasting technology, competitor analysis, and others. Despite the usefulness of

Shared vision must deal with the future.

these tools, by themselves they cannot produce a shared vision. Simply put, such tools fail to push you and your coworkers to seriously reconceive your jobs and the work environment. It is only when you do this, and in doing so become a futurist, that you really begin creating your future.

A shared vision is a statement of what will be created in the years ahead, and, therefore, obviously deals with the future. Of course that requires you to develop the ability to think long-term.

Creating a shared vision requires taking a stand for a preferred future.

By becoming a futurist, you should find it easier to project your thinking about a range of possible job and work environment futures in a systematic way. That, in turn, will stimulate you and your coworkers to develop a greater range of possible shared visions from which you can select the best.

Here are a few questions that can serve as catalysts in clarifying the future and developing your shared vision:

- If you could create the future, what future would you create for yourself, your job, and your work area or unit?

- How many categories of future developments can you currently identify that you believe will influence your job and vision statement?

- Can you make a list of expectations, based on the time frame of your vision statement, for each of the above categories?

- Can you prioritize a list of those expectations that would have the greatest impact on your vision statement?

PHASE III: CRAFTING A SHARED VISION

The time has come for you to put it all together—intuition, personal visions, experience, judgment, information, values, and culture—to create the shared vision that will distinguish you and your coworkers. To do this, the vision must be distinctive and establish standards that coworkers find necessary to follow. How do you do this? In crafting your shared vision, consider the following as a helpful model.

Put it all together to

create the shared vision

that will distinguish you.

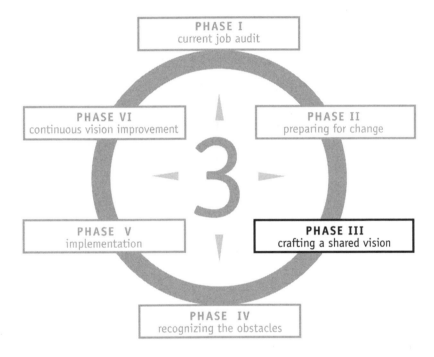

Step One: Knowledge is Important

Start by reviewing all the information and materials that you have compiled. In doing this, however, keep in mind that a significant source of this knowledge about your job and workplace is based on direct experience. From that experience you have gained invaluable information about what happens, how things happen, and who makes things happen in your unit and work environment.

Stay flexible and receptive.

The knowledge then becomes the source for much of the insight that goes into crafting your shared vision. At the same time, however, it is important at this early stage to stay flexible and receptive to ideas, intuition, and unique insights regardless of the source. Look for lots of ideas in places you may have been avoiding or otherwise ignoring.

Step Two: The Driving Force

Behind each job or position is a particular logic, force, element, or motive that distinguishes it from all others, giving it a special identity. The identification of what now drives the strategy and logic of your job and has pushed it in its current direction can be a key factor in considering your future direction and shared vision.

It is especially important that you know the driving logic or motive, especially if your shared vision is likely to change or have an impact on it. It will play a significant role in determining of your job's future and your vision.

Although as many as ten elements or areas can influence your job, only one emerges as the primary source of its driving force. The following is a list of representative key areas from which you should be able to identify that force or strategic logic:

Potential Driving Forces

- Products or service offered

- Users/customers

- Markets served

- Low-cost production, capability/capacity

- Marketing/sales methods

- Technology

- Method of distribution

- Return/profit

- Size/growth

- Natural resources

Behind each job or position is a particular force that distinguishes it and gives it a special identity.

Step Three: Rank the Options

Your next step is to develop a list of prioritized and tested shared visions that can produce success for you and your major constituent groups, and ultimately, the organization. Prioritize this list with the chief criteria being the most attractive and promising. When you complete the ranking, start at the top and test each one against Phase II, Preparing for Change, and other success factors that have been discussed. Finally, in your judgment, are your coworkers' and unit's strengths, driving force, culture, and values consistent? Is consistency important or is change a higher priority?

Step Four: Choose the Best

Finally, choose and state, as clearly as possible, the best shared vision for you and your coworkers from the prioritized list of possibilities. Keep in mind, however, that although intuition and experience may make the choice seem obvious, you are encouraged to test again against the key elements of a vision discussed earlier.

Vision focus. Once you are satisfied that this is the vision you really want, put it into a short, easily understood statement that focuses on and reflects:

- An exciting future

- The creation of value for you and your coworkers

- Standards of excellence that reflect high ideals, standards, and uniqueness to everyone that you and your coworkers interact with

- Clear criteria for decision making and evaluation

- Your enthusiasm and commitment

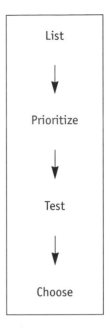

List

↓

Prioritize

↓

Test

↓

Choose

PHASE IV: RECOGNIZING THE OBSTACLES

The process of information collection, analysis, and judgment has led you to a choice for a new direction. At this point it would be wise to stop and reflect on the new shared vision by asking yourself:

- Is this the best vision?

- What are the chances for its success?

- If it fails, what can the unit salvage?

- Should we even try?

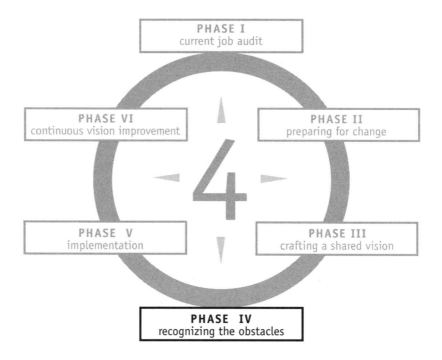

Do the Leaders Believe in The Vision?

It is important to ask questions in order to remove any doubts that your shared vision inspires commitment and enthusiasm. Do you really believe in it? Is it right for everyone who will interact with it, and will it lead to your own and your coworkers' improved performance?

Doubt and uncertainty are potential, even inevitable when a person embarks in a new direction. You can resolve this, however, by answering the following questions:

- Does everyone clearly understand the vision?

- How does your current situation compare with the new vision?

- How will the vision affect you and your coworkers?

- How will the vision affect your internal competition?

Does Everyone Clearly Understand the Vision?

Be certain that everyone who will be in contact with your new shared vision clearly understands it. Coworkers and managers commit to the vision only when they fully understand it. Although there are many ways to test for such understanding, here are three effective and commonly used methods.

Understanding is a critical step toward commitment.

1. Use a small group of people in your unit or work group whose views you value, and with whom you feel comfortable and can trust to be honest, as a sounding board.
2. Find ways to meet and talk informally and in relaxed conditions with managers, colleagues, customers, and suppliers about their understanding of your unit's vision.
3. There are formal ways to test the impact and understanding of the vision. Printed materials, such as memos, newsletters, and bulletin board displays, are very popular and offer an excellent way to develop understanding and commitment.

How Does Your Current Situation Compare with the New Shared Vision?

Take the time to give careful thought to a comparison of your new vision to your current work or job situation, including job description, work environment, unit/organization mission and purpose. The questions that need to be considered include:

- How far apart are your vision and the current work conditions?

- What changes, if any, will be required to make the transition to the new vision?

- Will your new vision require new or additional resources, technology, and skills?

- Is the time frame for its achievement realistic?

- Based on the answers to these and related questions, does the new shared vision need modification or revision?

How Will the Vision Affect You and Your Coworkers?

What are its chances

of success?

A fourth question also involves an important comparison. It consists of identifying differences or similarities between your vision and the information in the Current Job Assessment that focuses on the internal and external environment. For example:

- Does your new vision maximize particular strengths, and conversely, minimize weaknesses?

- Does the newly crafted shared vision challenge your work group's current culture?

- How well does the vision respond to current and future opportunities as well as threats?

How Will the Vision Affect Internal Competition?

Will your shared vision

enable you to control or

influence the internal

competitive arena?

The final question consists of determining which, if any, of your internal competitors will be attracted to your shared vision. Of course, if it reflects a significant change, it will naturally attract new competitors. More importantly, will your vision enable you and your coworkers to control or influence the competitive arena and the strategy of any new internal competitors as it had those in the past? The following questions bring these concerns into sharper focus:

- Does your vision challenge your internal competition's strength and exploit their weaknesses?

- What do you think your internal competition's reactions will be to your unit's shared vision and, if negative, can these actions be neutralized?

- Assuming they have one, what is each internal competitor's strategy or vision, and what is driving it?

- Does the new vision counteract the internal competitor's particular expertise and competence?

The questions and answers in this step reveal some critical issues that require attention and resolution if your shared vision is to become a successful reality. The issues, when resolved, provide a bridge between the old and new. Once you are satisfied with the answers, your vision is ready for implementation.

PHASE V: IMPLEMENTATION—VISION IN ACTION

Your vision statement is nothing more than a statement until it is put into action. Of course the words are very important, but it is only after it is put into action that it acquires the power to change your environment and move you and your coworkers in a new direction.

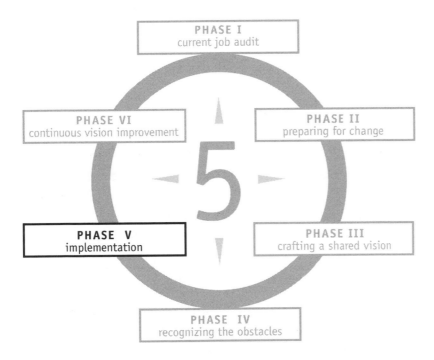

Action and Commitment

Putting the new vision into action presents you with the same challenges commonly associated with implementing any significant work or job change. It requires similar action and commitment. Action gives life to the new vision. Your commitment inspires coworkers and unit managers to buy in and understand what it means for them personally. As is the case with any attempt at change, the actions needed to implement your vision demand quality communication. These actions also encourage your managers to give priority to the allocation of time and resources needed to support the new direction.

If the vision is to become

reality, "you" must use it.

Keep in mind that if your shared vision is to become a reality, you and the unit must commit to using it. To get the commitment of your coworkers may even require persuading them to change their perceptions of what is important for them. Some useful considerations:

1. It is critical that you openly demonstrate by your actions a personal commitment to the vision. You must be ready to accept such roles as direction setter, change agent, communicator, and even coach. As a visionary leader, you must consistently apply the vision to all of your actions and decisions and look for opportunities to communicate it. Your purpose is to get the message across that using the vision is the thing to do.

   Keep in mind that communicating a shared vision to a selected group of coworkers or unit can present a challenge. In a complex or growing area of an organization, helping people comprehend the most recent plan, and their role in its implementation, can by itself be a daunting task. But attempting to get these same individuals to understand a vision of a new future presents a communication problem that is significantly greater in scope and challenge.

People need to know

that the shared vision

is working.

2. From the start, you must commit to communicating the significance of the vision to everyone. People need to know that it is working. Everyone affected by the vision must be constantly reminded that its success will propel the unit to the top in the organization. On a personal level, fellow employees need to know the level of commitment that you have made to the success of the vision. In addition, you should regularly announce and demonstrate the opportunities that the accomplishment of the shared vision holds for each coworker.

3. You are the primary communicator of the vision; it is doomed if your actions and words fail to reinforce it. From the beginning, you must be personally and directly involved in that task. You must enthusiastically commit to the vision. The next step involves getting a similar commitment from colleagues and supervisory staff. Rather than giving lip service to "empowerment," it is essential that you practice it. Coworkers will turn to you when they are looking for a role model as they observe the impact of the vision and begin applying it.

PHASE VI: CONTINUOUS VISION IMPROVEMENT

To keep a shared vision alive over a period of time, naturally requires periodic reviews and updates. These reevaluations and renewals provide a vital check on the unit's progress with implementation. Does the shared vision statement still have meaning in your job, your unit, and to you personally? Do the assumptions and judgments from which the vision sprang remain valid?

Does your shared vision statement still have meaning?

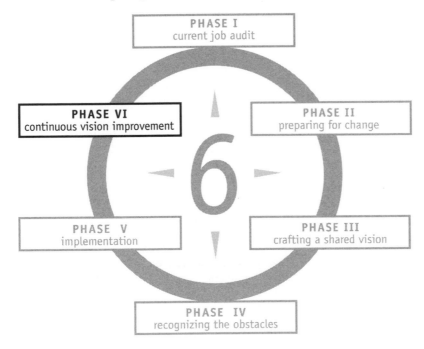

157

In addition, since all visions are by definition always just beyond reach, you must continuously refine and revise it to cope with critical issues generated by ongoing changes in your job responsibilities, work environment, or unit. As long as your shared vision can stay ahead of the rapidly changing times and technology, it needs reaffirmation and support.

Although no set rules say when to reevaluate a vision, it is usually done within six to twelve months of implementation. At this time, focus on the impact of changes in your personal and internal work environment and the monitoring of progress made on critical issues you have identified. After that, review the vision regularly, or as internal environmental factors appear that would threaten its success. Keep in mind that the vision-crafting process outlined earlier provides an excellent agenda for the review of potential changes in your vision. It must keep you, your job, and ultimately, your unit on the cutting edge of growth.

Shared vision must keep you, your job, and ultimately, your unit on the cutting edge of growth.

Summary

LOOKING BACK AT THE KEY POINTS of shared visioning and how you can make it happen, keep the following in mind:

- Visioning is the starting point for total quality management, process improvement, process management, continuous improvement, and reengineering.

- A thoughtfully created and implemented shared vision sustains your commitment to change throughout a change process.

- A vision statement captures an ideal, unique, and attractive image of your future and answers the question, "What do I want to create?"

- In addition to identifying and defining the new tomorrow, shared visioning provides the framework that guides decision making, planning, and action regarding the work situation.

- A shared vision is much more than a powerful tool—it is a strategy and mental attitude for expanding your personal horizons about what can be.

- For many leaders, a shared vision begins as a personal vision, a dream, a stroke of genius, or simply a "gut feeling." For others, it is born of either a combination of intuition and unique insight or a continuous and often chaotic process.

- While hard data may inform, it is soft data that provides the insights and wisdom on which to build an effective vision.

- Visioning starts with a clear understanding of the current composition, operation, and direction of your job, work environment, unit, and the fundamentals of the business you are in.

- The crafting of a shared vision that distinguishes you and your unit is the sum of intuition, personal visions, experiences, judgment, information, and values.

- Throughout the visioning process, pause and answer questions to remove any doubts you may feel that it inspires commitment and enthusiasm.

- While the words are very important, it is only after the shared vision is put into action that it acquires the power to change you and your job.

- To keep the vision alive and meaningful over a period of time requires periodic reviews and updates.

- The shared vision must keep you and your work on the cutting edge of growth.

Glossary of Terms

Champion: A key role for the visionary leader. As the embodiment of the organization's vision, the leader must demonstrate the vision as dramatically as possible in highly visible situations. As its champion, the leader both lives and constantly communicates the vision.

Change agent: Individual(s) who act as the catalyst for the organizational changes necessary to achieve the vision.

Coach: A critical role for the visionary leader. An effective coach is a team builder passionately committed to the vision as well as a mentor and role model for those whose efforts are needed to implement and achieve the vision.

Competitor assessment: An assessment that assists in determining how competitors affect the organization and its vision.

Constituencies (or stakeholders): A person, group, or institution that can influence the organization or that the organization can influence significantly. For most organizations, a list of constituents includes customers or users, competitors, suppliers, the external community, employees, managers, and owners or stockholders.

Continuous improvement: A key value or principle of total quality management, based on knowing where the organization is today, where it wants to be tomorrow, and challenging people to higher levels of success and achievement.

Current organization audit: An assessment that provides information on the basic nature of the organization and how it functions.

Driving force: The single most important force, element, or motive that drives the organization's strategy and gives it its particular identity.

Futurist: Individual who studies and forecasts future trends and developments.

Hard data: A source of information that is quantitative, historical, and objective. It is usually the result of long and exhaustive studies with a numerical base.

Macro-level training: Training designed to empower people to use the organization's vision and develop relevant skills.

Mission: A clearly defined and motivational statement that focuses on a goal toward which the organization will work.

Organization variables assessment: An assessment that focuses on people's experience and perceptions about key areas of the internal and external environment in which the organization functions.

Purpose: The basic set of reasons for the organization's existence. A statement of what the people in an organization want it to provide internally and externally.

Reengineering: The fundamental analysis and redesign of business processes to achieve dramatic improvements in performance through the use of current information technology. Reengineering focuses on innovative ways of doing business, managing people through such changes, and using the appropriate information technology to support the new environment.

Soft data: Qualitative information that is subjective, because it is based on personal perceptions, opinions, judgments, and feelings.

Strategic planning: A description of the steps an organization must take to achieve its vision.

Synergy: The working together of two or more elements, factors, or units to achieve an effect of which each is individually capable.

Total quality management (TQM): An integrated effort to improve products, services, and processes on a continuous basis. Everyone in the organization is involved. TQM requires a clear understanding of the relationship between an organization and all its stakeholders.

Values: A unique set of core beliefs, or abstract ideas that influences the direction, thinking, and actions of the organization.

Vision: A statement that captures an ideal, unique, and attractive image of an organization's future when challenged to answer the question, "What do we want to create?" Vision is the ability to see what is potential and what is necessary when confronted by opportunity. It clearly identifies where everyone agrees the organization is going and the major activities that will get it there.

Vision limitations: The time, geographic, political, socioeconomic and the organization's cultural restraints on the vision.

Vision needs assessment: An assessment to determine if conditions and timing require a new vision for the organization.

Vision skills assessment: An evaluation of the recognition, understanding, and application of the organization's vision.

Selected Readings

Agor, W., (ed.). *Intuition in Organizations: Leading and Managing Productively*. Thousand Oaks, Calif.: Sage Publications, 1989.

Armstrong, L. "Sony's Challenge." *Business Week* (June 1, 1987) 38-43.

Bennis, W., and Burt Nanus. *Leaders: The Strategy for Taking Charge*. New York: HarperCollins, 1986.

Bennis, W. "Leadership in the 21st Century." *Training* (May 1990) 231-234.

Block, P. *The Empowered Manager: Positive Political Skills at Work*. San Francisco: Jossey-Bass, 1987.

Bowles, J. "The Quality Imperative." *Fortune* (October 22, 1988) 126-128.

Browning, E. S. "Japanese Triumph: Sony's Perseverance Helped to Win Market for Mini-Compact Disk Player." *The Wall Street Journal* (February 27, 1986) 1.

Clifford, D. K., Jr., and R. E. Cavanagh. *The Winning Performance: How America's High-Growth Midsize Companies Succeed*. New York: Bantam Books, 1992.

Collins, J. C., and J. I. Porras. *Built to Last: Successful Habits of Visionary Companies*. Harper Business, 1994.

Collins, J. C., and J. I. Porras, "Building Your Company Vision." *Harper Business Review* (September-October 1996) 65-77.

Davis, S., and B. Davidson. *2020 Vision*. New York: Simon and Schuster, 1992.

Drucker, P. "Behind Japan's Success." *Harvard Business Review* (January-February 1981) 83-90.

Drucker, P. *Innovation and Entrepreneurship: Practices and Principles*. New York: Harper and Row, 1993.

Gilder, G. *Recapturing the Spirit of Enterprise*. New York: Simon and Schuster, 1992.

Hamel, G., and C. K. Prahalad. "Strategic Intent." *Harvard Business Review* (May-June 1989).

Hammer, M., and J. Champy. *Reengineering the Corporation: A Manifesto for Business Revolution*. New York: Harper Business, 1993.

Huey, J. "Wal-Mart: Will It Take Over the World?" *Fortune* (January 30, 1989) 52-64.

Hays, R. "Strategic Planning—Forward in Reverse?" *Harvard Business Review* (November-December 1985).

Imai, M. Kaizen: *The Key to Japan's Competitive Success*. New York: McGraw-Hill, 1986.

Kanter, R. M. *The Change Masters: Innovations for Productivity in the American Corporation*. New York: Simon and Schuster, 1983.

Kikuchi, M. *Japanese Electronics: A Worm's-Eye View of Its Evolution*. Tokyo: Simul, 1983.

Kotler, P., W. Fahey, and S. Jatusriditak. *The New Competition*. Englewood Cliffs, N.J.: Prentice-Hall, 1991.

Kotter, J. *A Force for Change: How Leadership Differs from Management.* New York: The Free Press, 1990.

Levinson, H., and S. Rosenthal. *CEO: Corporate Leadership in Action.* New York: Basic Books, 1984.

Love, J. F. *McDonald's—Behind the Arches.* New York: Bantam, 1995.

Main, J. "Wanted: Leaders Who Can Make A Difference." *Fortune* (September 28, 1987) 92.

Mintzberg, H., and J. Quinn. "Honda Motor Company" (case). *The Strategy Process*, second ed. Englewood Cliffs, N.J.: Prentice Hall, 1992.

Mintzberg, H. *Mintzberg on Management: Inside Our Strange World of Organizations.* New York: Free Press, 1989.

Mintzberg, H. *The Rise and Fall of Strategic Planning: Reconceiving Roles For Planning, Plans, Planners.* New York: Free Press, 1994.

Morgan, G. *Riding The Waves of Change: Developing Managerial Competencies for A Turbulent World.* San Francisco: Jossey-Bass, 1988.

Naisbitt, J., and P. Aburdene. *Reinventing The Corporation Future: Transforming your Job and Your Company for the New Information Society.* New York: Warner Books, 1992.

Nanus, B. "QUEST—Quick Environment Scanning Technique." *Long Range Planning* (April 1982).

Nanus, B. *Visionary Leadership: Creating a Compelling Sense of Direction for Your Organization.* San Francisco: Jossey-Bass, 1992.

Pascale, R. T. "Perspectives on Strategy: the Real Story Behind Honda's Success." *California Management Review* (Spring 1984) 47-74.

Pascale, R. T. and A. G. Athos. *The Art of Japanese Management.* New York: Simon and Schuster, 1981.

Peters, T. *Liberation Management: Necessary Disorganization for the Nanosecond Nineties.* New York: Knopf, 1994.

Powers, C. "At Johnson and Johnson, A Mistake Can Be a Badge af Honor." *Business Week* (September 26, 1988), 126-128.

Quinn, J. B. *Intelligent Enterprise.* New York: Free Press, 1992.

Quinn, J. B., H. Mintzberg, and R.M. James. *The Strategy Process.* Englewood Cliffs, N.J.: Prentice-Hall, 1993.

Ronch, S. "Services Under Siege: The Restructuring Imperative." *Harvard Business Review* (September-October 1991).

Rowan, R. *The Intuitive Manager.* New York: Berkley Publications, 1991.

Scott, B. R. "Competitiveness: 23 Leaders Speak Out." *Harvard Business Review* (July-August 1987) 106-123.

Senge, P. *The Fifth Discipline: The Art and Practice of the Learning Organization.* New York: Doubleday, 1990.

Stacey, R. D. *Managing the Unknowable: Strategic Boundaries Between Order and Chaos in Organizations.* San Francisco: Jossey-Bass, 1992.

Tichy, N. M., and M.A. Devanna. *The Transformational Leader.* New York: John Wiley and Sons, 1986.

Tregoe, B. B., J.W. Zimmerman, R. A. Smith and P. M. Tobia. *Vision In Action.* New York: Simon and Schuster, 1994.

Vaill, P. B. *Managing as A Performing Art: New Ideas for a World of Chaotic Change.* New York: McGraw-Hill, 1991.

About the Author

C. PATRICK LEWIS is Training Manager, Training Division, The QuickSilver Group, Inc., specializing in custom design and development training solutions for technology-based enterprises. Patrick was co-founder and Vice President of C. D. Lewis and Associates, Inc., a successful custom training design and development company that merged with The QuickSilver Group, Inc. With over thirty years of experience as an educator, administrator, and manager, he has applied his knowledge and skills to a wide variety of organization, management, and leadership issues. His consulting interests and specialties include Organizational Visioning, Visioning Skills Development, Strategic Management, and Strategic Organization Diagnosis.

BOOKS FROM PRODUCTIVITY, INC.

Productivity, Inc. publishes books that empower individuals and companies to achieve excellence in quality, productivity, and the creative involvement of all employees. Through steadfast efforts to support the vision and strategy of continuous improvement, Productivity delivers today's leading-edge tools and techniques gathered directly from industry leaders around the world. Call toll-free 1-800-394-6868 for our free catalog.

20 KEYS TO WORKPLACE IMPROVEMENT (Revised Edition)
Iwao Kobayashi

The 20 Keys system does more than just bring together twenty of the world's top manufacturing improvement approaches–it integrates these individual methods into a closely interrelated system for revolutionizing every aspect of your manufacturing organization. This revised edition of Kobayashi's bestseller amplifies the synergistic power of raising the levels of all these critical areas simultaneously. The new edition presents upgraded criteria for the five-level scoring system in most of the 20 Keys, supporting your progress toward becoming not only best in your industry, but best in the world. New material and an updated layout throughout assist managers in implementing this comprehensive approach. In addition, valuable case studies describe how Morioka Seiko (Japan) advanced in Key 18 (use of microprocessors) and how Windfall Products (Pennsylvania) adapted the 20 Keys to its situation with good results.
ISBN 1-56327-109-5/ 312 pages / $50.00 / Order 20KREV-B271

THE BENCHMARKING MANAGEMENT GUIDE
American Productivity & Quality Center

If you're planning, organizing, or actually undertaking a benchmarking program, you need the most authoritative source of information to help you get started and to manage the process all the way through. Written expressly for managers of benchmarking projects by the APQC's renowned International Benchmarking Clearinghouse, this guide provides exclusive information from members who have already paved the way. It includes information on training courses and ways to apply Baldrige, Deming, and ISO 9000 criteria for internal assessment. Included is a complete bibliography of benchmarking literature.
ISBN 1-56327-045-5 / 260 pages / $40.00 / Order BMG-B271

CORPORATE DIAGNOSIS
Setting the Global Standard for Excellence
Thomas L. Jackson with Constance E. Dyer

All too often, strategic planning neglects the essential first and final steps: Diagnosis of the organization's current state. What's required is a systematic review of the critical factors in organizational learning and growth, factors that require monitoring, measurement, and management to ensure that your company competes successfully. This executive workbook provides a step-by-step method for diagnosing an organization's strategic health and measuring its overall competitiveness against world class standards. With checklists, charts, and detailed explanations, *Corporate Diagnosis* is a practical instruction manual. The pillars of Jackson's diagnostic system are strategy, structure, and capability. Detailed diagnostic questions in each area are provided as guidelines for developing your own self-assessment survey.

ISBN 1-56327-086-2 / 100 pages / $65.00 / Order CDIAG-B271

FEEDBACK TOOLKIT
16 Tools for Better Communication in the Workplace
Rick Maurer

In companies striving to reduce hierarchy and foster trust and responsible participation, good person-to-person feedback can be as important as sophisticated computer technology in enabling effective teamwork. Feedback is an important map of your situation, a way to tell whether you are "on or off track." Used well, feedback can motivate people to their highest level of performance. Despite its significance, this level of information sharing makes most managers uncomfortable. *Feedback Toolkit* addresses this natural hesitation with an easy-to-grasp six-step framework and 16 practical and creative approaches for giving and receiving feedback with individuals and groups. Maurer's reality-tested methods in *Feedback Toolkit* are indispensable equipment for managers and teams in every organization.

ISBN 1-56327-056-0 / 109 pages / $12.00 / Order FEED-B271

HANDBOOK FOR PRODUCTIVITY MEASUREMENT AND IMPROVEMENT
William F. Christopher and Carl G. Thor, eds.

An unparalleled resource! In over 100 chapters, nearly 80 front-runners in the quality movement reveal the evolving theory and specific practices of world class organizations. Spanning a wide variety of industries and business sectors, they discuss quality and productivity in manufacturing, service industries, profit centers, administration, nonprofit and government institutions, health care and education. Contributors include Robert C. Camp, Peter F. Drucker, Jay W. Forrester, Joseph M. Juran, Robert S. Kaplan, John W. Kendrick, Yasuhiro Monden, and Lester C. Thurow. Comprehensive in scope and organized for easy reference, this compendium belongs in every company and academic institution concerned with business and industrial viability.
ISBN 1-56327-007-2 / 1344 pages / $90.00 / Order HPM-B271

HANDBOOK OF STRATEGIES AND TOOLS FOR THE LEARNING COMPANY
C. Carl Pegels

This book combines the best of management strategies, from the tried and true techniques to new innovations, into a comprehensive management resource. It covers such topics as employee empowerment, teams, and product management using real-world examples from companies including IBM, Ford, and Saturn.
ISBN 1-56327-2105 / 496 pages / $65.00 / Order PEGELS-B271

THE HUNTERS AND THE HUNTED
A Non-Linear Solution for Reengineering the Workplace
James B. Swartz

Our competitive environment changes rapidly. If you want to survive, you have to stay on top of those changes. Otherwise, you become prey to your competitors. Hunters continuously change and learn; anyone who doesn't becomes the hunted and sooner or later will be devoured. This unusual non-fiction novel provides a veritable crash course in continuous transformation. It offers lessons from real-life companies and introduces many industrial gurus as characters. *The Hunters and the Hunted* doesn't simply tell you how to change; it puts you inside the change process itself.
ISBN 1-56327-043-9 / 582 pages / $45.00 / Order HUNT-B271

IMPLEMENTING A LEAN MANAGEMENT SYSTEM
Thomas L. Jackson with Karen R. Jones

Does your company think and act ahead of technological change, ahead of the customer, and ahead of the competition? Thinking strategically requires a company to face these questions with a clear future image of itself. *Implementing a Lean Management System* lays out a comprehensive management system for aligning the firm's vision of the future with market realities. Based on hoshin management, the Japanese strategic planning method used by top managers for driving TQM throughout an organization, *Lean Management* is about deploying vision, strategy, and policy to all levels of daily activity. It is an eminently practical methodology emerging out of the implementation of continuous improvement methods and employee involvement. The key tools of this book build on the knowledge of the worker, multiskilling, and an understanding of the role and responsibilities of the new lean manufacturer.
ISBN 1-56327-085-4 / 182 pages / $65.00 / Order ILMS-B271

IMPLEMENTING TPM
The North American Experience
Charles J. Robinson and Andrew P. Ginder

This book offers a modified approach to TPM planning and deployment that builds on the 12-step process advocated by the Japan Institute of Plant Maintenance. More than just an implementation guide, it's actually a testimonial of proven TPM success in North American companies through the adoption of "best in class" manufacturing practices. Of special interest are chapters on implementing TPM in union environments, integrating benchmarking practices to support TPM, and a requirements checklist for computerized maintenance management systems.
ISBN 1-56327-087-0 / 224 pages / $45.00 / Order IMPTPM-B271

LEARNING ORGANIZATIONS
Developing Cultures for Tomorrow's Workplace
Sarita Chawla and John Renesch, eds.

The ability to learn faster than your competition may be the only sustainable competitive advantage. A learning organization is one where people continually expand their capacity to create results they truly desire, where new and expansive patterns of thinking are nurtured, where collective aspiration is set free, and where people are continually learning how to learn together. This compilation of 34 powerful essays, written by recognized experts worldwide, is rich in concept and theory as well as application and example. An inspiring follow-up to Peter Senge's groundbreaking bestseller *The Fifth Discipline*, these essays are grouped in four sections that address all aspects of learning organizations: the guiding ideas behind systems thinking; the theories, methods, and processes for creating a learning organization; the infrastructure of the learning model; and arenas of practice.
ISBN 1-56327-110-9 / 575 pages / $35.00 / Order LEARN-B271

A NEW AMERICAN TQM
Four Practical Revolutions in Management
Shoji Shiba, Alan Graham, and David Walden

For TQM to succeed in America, you need to create an American-style "learning organization" with the full commitment and understanding of senior managers and executives. Written expressly for this audience, *A New American TQM* offers a comprehensive and detailed explanation of TQM and how to implement it, based on courses taught at MIT's Sloan School of Management and the Center for Quality Management, a consortium of American companies. Full of case studies and amply illustrated, the book examines major quality tools and how they are being used by the most progressive American companies today.
ISBN 1-56327-032-3 / 606 pages / $50.00 / Order NATQM-B271

A REVOLUTION IN MANUFACTURING
The SMED System
Shigeo Shingo

The heart of JIT is quick changeover methods. Dr. Shingo, inventor of the Single-Minute Exchange of Die (SMED) system for Toyota, shows you how to reduce your changeovers by an average of 98 percent! By applying Shingo's techniques, you'll see rapid improvements (lead time reduced from weeks to days, lower inventory and warehousing costs) that will improve quality, productivity, and profits.
ISBN 0-915299-03-8 / 383 pages / $75.00 / Order SMED-B271

SECRETS OF A SUCCESSFUL EMPLOYEE RECOGNITION SYSTEM
Daniel C. Boyle

As the human resource manager of a failing manufacturing plant, Dan Boyle was desperate to find a way to motivate employees and break down the barrier between management and the union. He came up with a simple idea—say thank you to you employees for doing their job. In *Secrets to a Successful Employee Recognition System*, Boyle outlines how to begin and run a 100 Club program. Filled with case studies and detailed guidelines, this book underscores the power behind thanking your employees for a job well done.
ISBN 1-56327-083-8 / 250 pages / $25.00 / Order SECRET-B271

STEPPING UP TO ISO 14000
Integrating Environmental Quality with ISO 9000 and TQM
Subash C. Puri

The newest ISO standards, announced in mid-1996, require environmentally-friendly practices in every aspect of a manufacturing business, from factory design and raw material acquisition to the production, packaging, distribution, and ultimate disposal of the product. Here's a comprehensible overview and implementation guide to the standards that's also the only one to show how they fit with current ISO 9000 efforts and other companywide programs for Total Quality Management (TQM).
ISBN 1-56327-129-X / 280 pages / $39.00 / Order SPTISO-B271

TOOL NAVIGATOR
The Master Guide for Teams
Walter J. Michalski

Are you constantly searching for just the right tool to help your team efforts? Do you find yourself not sure which to use next? Here's the largest tool compendium of facilitation and problem solving tools you'll find. Each tool is presented in a two to three page spread which describes the tool, its use, how to implement it, and an example. Charts provide a matrix to help you choose the right tool for your needs. Plus, you can combine tools to help your team navigate through any problem solving or improvement process. Use these tools for all seasons: team building, idea generating, data collecting, analyzing/trending, evaluating/selecting, decision making, planning/presenting, and more!
ISBN 1-56327-178-8 / 550 pages / $150.00 / Order NAVI1-B271

THE UNSHACKLED ORGANIZATION
Facing the Challenge of Unpredictability Through Spontaneous Reorganization
Jeffrey Goldstein

Managers should not necessarily try to solve all the internal problems within their organizations. Intervention may help in the short term, but in the long run may inhibit true problem-solving change from taking place. And change is the real goal. Through change comes real hope for improvement. Using leading-edge scientific and social theories about change, Goldstein explores how change happens within an organization and reveals that only through "self-organization" can natural, lasting change occur. This book is a pragmatic guide for managers, executives, consultants, and other change agents.
ISBN 1-56327-048-X / 208 pages / $25.00 / Order UO-B271

TO ORDER: Write, phone, or fax Productivity, Inc., Dept. BK, P.O. Box 13390, Portland, OR 97213-0390, phone 1-800-394-6868, fax 1-800-394-6286. Send check or charge to your credit card (American Express, Visa, MasterCard accepted).

U.S. ORDERS: Add $5 shipping for first book, $2 each additional for UPS surface delivery. Add $5 for each AV program containing 1 or 2 tapes; add $12 for each AV program containing 3 or more tapes. We offer attractive quantity discounts for bulk purchases of individual titles; call for more information.

ORDER BY E-MAIL: Order 24 hours a day from anywhere in the world. Use either address:
To order: **service@productivityinc.com**
To view the online catalog and/or order: **http://www.productivityinc.com**

QUANTITY DISCOUNTS: For information on quantity discounts, please contact our sales department.

INTERNATIONAL ORDERS: Write, phone, or fax for quote and indicate shipping method desired. For international callers, telephone number is 503-235-0600 and fax number is 503-235-0909. Prepayment in U.S. dollars must accompany your order (checks must be drawn on U.S. banks). When quote is returned with payment, your order will be shipped promptly by the method requested.

NOTE: Prices are in U.S. dollars and are subject to change without notice.